# TRAVELS IN MOROCCO,

BY THE LATE

## JAMES RICHARDSON,

AUTHOR OF "A MISSION TO CENTRAL AFRICA," "TRAVELS IN THE DESERT OF SAHARA," &C.

### EDITED BY HIS WIDOW.

IN TWO VOLUMES.

VOL. II.

LONDON:
CHARLES J. SKEET, PUBLISHER,
10, KING WILLIAM STREET,
CHARING CROSS.
1860.

LONDON:
Printed by A. Schulze, 13, Poland Street.

# CONTENTS

OF

# THE SECOND VOLUME.

## CHAPTER I.

Page

The Mogador Jewesses.—Disputes between the Jew and the Moor.—Melancholy Scenes.—The Jews of the Atlas.—Their Religion.—Beautiful Women.—The Four Wives.—Statues discovered.—Discrepancy in the age of Married People.—Young and frail fair ones.—Superstition respecting Salt.—White Brandy.—Ludicrous Anecdote.  . . . . . . 1

## CHAPTER II.

The Maroquine dynasties.—Family of the Shereefian Monarchs.—Personal appearance and character of Muley Abd Errahman.—Refutation of the charge of human sacrifices against the Moorish Princes.—Genealogy of the reigning dynasty of Morocco.—The tyrant Yezeed, (half Irish).—Muley Suleiman, "The Shereef of Shereefs."—Diplomatic relations of the Emperor of Morocco with European Powers.—Muley Ismael enamoured with the French Princess de Conti.—Rival diplomacy of France and England near the Maroquine Court.—Mr. Hay's correspondence with this Court on the Slave-trade.—Treaties between Great Britain and Morocco; how defective and requiring amendment.—Unwritten engagements. . . - . . . 23

## CHAPTER III.

The two different aspects by which the strength and resources of the Empire of Morocco may be viewed or estimated.—Native appellation of Morocco.—Geographical limits of this country.—Historical review of the inhabitants of North Africa, and the manner in which this region was successively peopled and conquered.—The distinct varieties of the human race, as found in Morocco.—Nature of the soil and climate of this country.—Derem, or the Atlas chain of mountains.—Natural products.—The Shebbel, or Barbary salmon; different characters of exports of the Northern and Southern provinces.—The Elæonderron Argan.—Various trees and plants.—Mines.—The Sherb-errech, or Desert-horse. . . . . 64

## CHAPTER IV.

Division of Morocco into kingdoms or States, and zones or regions.—Description of the towns and cities on the Maroquine coasts of the Mediterranean and Atlantic waters.—The Zafarine Isles.—Melilla.—Alhucemas. —Penon de Velez.—Tegaza.—Provinces of Rif and Garet. — Tetouan. — Ceuta. — Arzila.— El Araish.— Mehedia.—Salee.—Rabat.—Fidallah.—Dar-el-Beidah. —Azamour.—Mazagran.—Saffee.—Waladia. . . 99

CONTENTS. v

## CHAPTER V.

Description of the Imperial Cities or Capitals of the Empire.—El-Kesar.—Mequinez.—Fez.—Morocco.—The province of Tafilett, the birth-place of the present dynasty of the Shereefs. . . . . . . 133

## CHAPTER VI.

Description of the towns and cities of the Interior, and those of the Kingdom of Fez.—Seisouan.—Wazen.—Zawiat.—Muley Dris.—Sofru.—Dubdu.—Taza.—Oushdah.—Agla.—Nakhila.—Meshra.—Khaluf.—The Places distinguished in Morocco, including Sous, Draha, and Tafilett.—Tefza.—Pitideb.—Ghuer.—Tyijet.—Bulawan.—Soubeit.—Meramer.—El-Medina.—Tagodast.—Dimenet.—Aghmat.—Fronga.—Tedmest.—Tekonlet.—Tesegdelt.—Tagawost.—Tedsi Beneali.—Beni Sabih.—Tatta and Akka.—Mesah or Assah.—Talent.—Shtouka.—General observations on the statistics of population.—The Maroquine Sahara. 159

## CHAPTER VII.

Lond : Jew-boys.—Excursion to the Emperor's garden, and the Argan Forests.—Another interview with the Governor of Mogador on the Anti-Slavery Address.—Opinion of the Moors on the Abolition of Slavery. . 186

## CHAPTER VIII.

El-Jereed, the Country of Dates.—Its hard soil.—Salt Lake.—Its vast extent.—Beautiful Palm-trees.—The Dates, a staple article of Food.—Some Account of the

Date-Palm.—Mode of Culture.—Delicious Beverage.—Tapping the Palm.—Meal formed from the Dates—Baskets made of the Branches of the Tree.—Poetry of the Palm.—Its Irrigation—Palm-Groves.—Collection of Tribute by the "Bey of the Camp." . . 200

## CHAPTER IX.

Tour in the Jereed of Captain Balfour and Mr. Reade.—Sidi-Mohammed.—Plain of Manouba.—Tfeefleah.—The Bastinado.—Turkish Infantry.—Kairwan.—Sidi Amour Abeda.—Saints.—A French Spy.—Administration of Justice.—The Bey's Presents.—The Hobara.—Ghafsa.—Hot streams containing Fish.—Snake.—Incantation.—Moorish Village. . . . . 215

## CHAPTER X.

Toser.—The Bey's Palace.—Blue Doves.—The town described.—Industry of the People.—Sheikh Tahib imprisoned and punished.—Leghma.—The Boohabeeba.—A Domestic Picture.—The Bey's Diversions.—The Bastinado.—Concealed Treasure.—Nefta.—The Two Saints.—Departure of Santa Maria.—Snake-charmers.—Wedyen.—Deer-Stalking.—Splendid view of the Sahara.—Revolting Acts.—Ghortabah.—Ghafsa.—Byrlafee.—Mortality among the Camels.—Aqueduct.—Remains of Udina.—Arrival at Tunis.—The Boab's Wives.—Curiosities.—Tribute Collected.—Author takes leave of the Governor of Mogador, and embarks for England.—Rough Weather.—Arrival in London. . . . . . 262

Appendix . . . . . . . 303

# TRAVELS IN MOROCCO.

## CHAPTER I.

The Mogador Jewesses.—Disputes between the Jew and the Moor.—Melancholy Scenes.—The Jews of the Atlas.—Their Religion.—Beautiful Women.—The Four Wives.—Statues discovered.—Discrepancy of age of married people.—Young and frail fair ones.—Superstition respecting Salt.—White Brandy.—Ludicrous Anecdote.

Notwithstanding the imbecile prejudices of the native Barbary Jews, such of them who adopt European habits, or who mix with European merchants, are tolerably good members of society, always endeavouring to restrain their own peculiarities. The European Jewesses settled in Mogador, are indeed the belles of society, and attend all the balls (such as they are). The Jewess sooner forgets religious differences than the Jew, and I was told by a Christian lady, it would be a dangerous matter for a Christian gentleman to make an offer of marriage to a Mogador Jewess, unless in downright earnest, as it would be sure to be accepted.

Monsieur Delaport, Consul of France, was the first official person who brought prominently forward the native and other Jews into the European society of this place, and since then, these Jews have improved in their manners, and increased their respectability. The principal European Jews are from London, Gibraltar, and Marseilles. Many native Jews have attempted to wear European clothes; and a European hat, or coat, is now the rage among native Jewesses, who all aspire to get a husband wearing either. Such are elements of the progress of the Jewess population in this part of the world, and there is no doubt their position has been greatly ameliorated within the last half century, or since the time of Ali Bey, who thus describes their wretched condition in his days.

" Continual disputes arise between the Jew and the Moor; when the Jew is wrong, the Moor takes his own satisfaction, and if the Jew be right, he lodges a complaint with the judge, who always decides in favour of the Mussulman. I have seen the Mahometan children amuse themselves by beating little Jews, who durst not defend themselves. When a Jew passes a mosque, he is obliged to take off his slippers, or shoes; he must do the same when he passes the house of the Kaëd, the Kady, or any Mussulman of distinction. At Fez, and in some other towns, they are obliged to walk barefooted." Ali Bey mentions other vexations and oppressions, and adds, " When I saw the Jews were so ill-treated and vexed in every way, I asked them why they did not go to another country. They answered that they could not do so, because they were slaves of the Sultan." Again he says, " As the Jews have a particular skill in thieving, they indemnify themselves for the ill-treatment they receive from the Moors, by cheating them daily."

Jewesses are exempt from taking off their slippers, or sandals, when passing the mosques. The late Emperor, Muley Suleiman,* professed to be a rigidly exact Mussulman, and considered it very indecent, and a great scandal that Jewesses, some of them, like most women of this country, of enormous dimensions, should be allowed to disturb the decent frame of mind of pious Mussulmen, whilst entering the threshold of the house of prayer, by the sad exhibitions of these good ladies stooping down and shewing their tremendous calves, when in the act of taking off their shoes before passing the mosques. For such reasons, Jewesses are now privileged and exempted from the painful necessity of walking barefoot in the streets.

* The predecessor of Muley Abd Errahman.

The policy of the Court in relation to the Jews continually fluctuates. Sometimes, the Emperor thinks they ought to be treated like the rest of his subjects; at other times, he seems anxious to renew in all its vigour the system described by Ali Bey. Hearing that the Jews of Tangier, on returning from Gibraltar, would often adopt the European dress, and so, by disguising themselves, be treated like Christians and Europeans, he ordered all these would-be Europeans forthwith to be undressed, and to resume their black turban.

Alas, how were all these Passover, Tabernacle and wedding festivals, these happy and joyous days of the Jewish society of Mogador, changed on the bombardment of that city! What became of the rich and powerful merchants, the imperial vassals of commerce with their gorgeous wives bending under the weight of diamonds, pearls, and precious gems, during that sad and unexpected period? The newspapers of the day recorded the melancholy story. Many of the

Jews were massacred, or buried underneath the ruins of the city; their wives subjected to plunder; the rest were left wandering naked and starving on the desolate sandy coast of the Atlantic, or hidden in the mountains, obtaining a momentary respite from the rapacious fury of the savage Berbers and Arabs.

It is well known that, while the French bombarded Tangier and Mogador from without, the Berber and Arab tribes, aided by the *canaille* of the Moors, plundered the city from within. Several of the Moorish rabble declared publicly, and with the greatest cowardice and villainous effrontery, " When the French come to destroy Mogador, we shall go and pillage the Jews' houses, strip the women of their ornaments, and then escape to the mountains from the pursuit of the Christians." These threats they faithfully executed; but, by a just vengeance, they were pillaged in turn, for the Berbers not only plundered the Jews themselves, but the Moors who had escaped from the city laden with their booty.

It is to be hoped that a better day is dawning for North African Jews. The Governments of France and England can do much for them in Morocco.

The Jews of the Atlas formed the subject of some of Mr. Davidson's literary labours; I have made further inquiries and shall give the reader some account of them, adding that portion of Mr. Davidson's information which was borne out by further investigation. The Atlas Jews are physically, if not morally, superior to their brethren who reside among the Moors. They are dispersed over the Atlas ranges, and have all the characteristics of mountaineers. They enjoy, like their neighbours, the Berbers and Shelouhs, a species of quasi-independence of the Imperial authority, but they usually attach themselves to certain Berber chieftains who protect them, and whose standards they follow.

These are the only Jews in Mahometan countries of whom I have heard as bearing arms. They have, however, their own Sheiks, to whose jurisdiction all domestic matters are referred. They wear the same attire as the mountaineers, and are not distinguishable from them, they do not address the Moors by the term of respect and title "Sidi," but in the same way as the Moors and Arabs when they accost each other. They speak the Shelouh language.

Mr. Davidson mentions some curious circumstances about these Jews, and of their having a city beyond the Atlas, where three or four thousand are living in perfect freedom, and cultivating the soil, which they have possessed since the time of Solomon. The probability is that Mr. Davidson's informant refers to the Jews of the Oasis of Sahara, where there certainly are some families of Jews living in comparative freedom and independence.

As to the peculiarities of the religion of the Atlas Jews, they are said not to have the Pentateuch and the law in the same order as

Jews generally. They are unacquainted with Ezra, or Christ; they did not go to Babylon at the captivity, but were dispersed over Africa at that period. They are a species of Caraaites, or Jewish Protestants. Shadai is the name which they apply to the Supreme Being, when speaking of him. Their written law begins by stating that the world was many thousand years old when the present race of men was formed, which, curiously enough, agrees with the researches of modern geology. The present race of men are the joint offspring of different and distinct human species. The deluge is not mentioned by them. God, it is said, appeared to Ishmael in a dream, and told him he must separate from Isaac, and go to the desert, where he would make him a great nation. There would ever after be enmity between the two races, as at this day there is the greatest animosity between the Jews and Mahometans.

The great nucleus of these Shelouh Jews

is in *Jebel Melge,* or the vast ridge of the Atlas capped with eternal snows; and they hold communications with the Jews of Ait Mousa, Frouga or Misfuvâ. They rarely descend to the plains or cities of the empire, and look upon the rest of the Jews of this country as heretics. Isolation thus begets enmity and mistrust, as in other cases. A few years ago, a number came to Mogador, and were not at all pleased with their visit, finding fault with everything among their brethren. These Jewish mountaineers are supposed to be very numerous. In their homes, they are inaccessible. So they live in a wild independence, professing a creed as free as their own mountain airs. God, who made the hills, made likewise man's freedom to abide therein. Before taking leave of the Maroquine Israelites, I must say something of their personal appearance. Both in Tangier and Mogador, I was fortunate enough to be acquainted with families, who could boast of the most perfect and classic types of Jewish female loveliness. Alas, that these beauties should be only charming *animals*, their minds and affections being left uncultivated, or converted into caves of unclean and tormenting passions. The Jewesses, in general, until they become enormously stout and weighed down with obesity, are of extreme beauty. Most of them have fair complexions; their rose and jasmine faces, their pure wax-like delicate features, and their exceedingly expressive and bewitching eyes, would fascinate the most fastidious of European connoisseurs of female beauty.

But these Israelitish ladies, recalling the fair image of Rachel in the Patriarchal times of Holy Writ, and worthy to serve as models for a Grecian sculptor, are treated with savage disdain by the churlish Moors, and sometimes are obliged to walk barefoot and prostrate themselves before their ugly negress concubines. The male infants of Jews are engaging and good-looking when young; but, as they grow up, they become ordinary; and Jews of a certain age, are decidedly and most disgustingly ugly. It is possible that the degrading slavery in which they usually live, their continued habits of cringing servility, by which the countenance acquires a sinister air and fiendishly cunning smirk, may cause this change in their appearance. But what contrasts we had of the beauty of countenance and form in the Jewish society of Mogador! You frequently see a youthful woman, nay a girl of exquisite beauty and delicacy of features, married to an old wretched ill-looking fellow of some sixty or seventy years of age, tottering over the grave, or an incurable invalid. To render them worse-looking, whilst the women may dress in any and the gayest colours, the men wear a dark blue and black turban and dress, and though this is prescribed as a badge of oppression, they will often assume it when they may attire themselves in white and other livelier colours. However, men get used to their misery, and hug their chains.

The Jews, at times, though but very rarely, avail themselves of their privilege of four wives granted them in Mahometan countries, and a nice mess they make of it. I knew a Jew of this description in Tunis. He was a lively, jocose fellow, with a libidinous countenance, singing always some catch of a song. He was a silk-mercer, and pretty well off. His house was small, and besides a common *salle-à-manger*, divided into four compartments for his four wives, each defending her room with the ferocity of a tigress. Two of them were of his own age, about fifty, and two not more than twenty. The two elder ones, I was told by his neighbours, were entirely abandoned by the husband, and the two younger ones were always bickering and quarrelling, as to which of them should have the greater favour of their common tyrant; the house a scene of tumult, disorder and indecency. Amongst the whole of the wives, there was only one child, a boy, of course an immense pet, a little surly wretch; his growth smothered, his health nearly ruined, by the over-attentions of the four women, whom he kicked and pelted when out of humour.

This little imp was the fit type, or interpretation of the presiding genius of polygamy. I once visited this happy family, this biting satire on domestic bliss and the beauty of the harem of the East. The women were all sour, and busy at work, weaving or spinning cotton, "Do you work for your husband?" I asked,

*The women.*—" Thank Rabbi, no."

*Traveller.*—" What do you do with your money?"

*The women.*—" Spend it ourselves."

*Traveller.*—" How do you like to have only one husband among you four?"

*The women.*—" Pooh! is it not the will of God?"

*Traveller.*—" Whose boy is that?"

*The women.*—" It belongs to us all."

*Traveller.*—" Have you no other children?"

*The women.*—Our husband is good for no more than that."

Whilst I was talking to these angelic creatures, their beloved lord was quietly stuffing capons, without hearing our polite discourse. A European Jew who knew the native society of Jews well, represents domestic bliss to be a mere phantom, and scarcely ever thought of, or sought after. Poor human nature!

I took a walk round the suburbs one morning, whilst a strong wind was bringing the locusts towards the coast, which fell upon us like hailstones. Young locusts frequently crowd upon the neighbouring hills in thousands and tens of thousands. They are little green things. No one knows whence they come and whither they go. These are not destructive. Indeed, unless swarms of locusts appear darkening the sky, and full grown ones, they do not permanently damage the country. The wind usually disperses them; they rarely take a long flight, except impelled by a violent gale. Arabs attempt to destroy locusts by digging pits into which they may fall. This is merely playing with them. Jews fry them in oil and salt, and sell them as we sell shrimps, the taste of which they resemble.

On my return, I passed a Mooress, or rather a Mauritanian Venus, who was so stout that she had fallen down, and could not get up. A mule was fetched to carry her home. But the Moor highly relishes these enormous lumps of fat, according to the standard beauty laid down by the talebs—" Four things in a woman should be ample, the lower part of the back, the thighs, the calves of the legs and the knees."

Some time ago, there were discovered at Malta various rude statues of women very ample in the lower part of the " back," supposed to be of Libyan origin, so that stout ladies have been the choicest of the fashion for ages past; the fattening of women, like so many capons and turkeys, begins when they are betrothed.

They then swallow three times a day regular

boluses of paste, and are not allowed to take exercise. By the time marriage takes place, they are in a tolerable good condition, not unlike Smithfield fattened heifers. The lady of one of the European merchants being very thin, the Moors frequently asked her husband how it was, and whether she had enough to eat, hinting broadly that he starved her.

On the other hand, two or three of the merchant's wives were exceedingly stout, and of course great favourites with the men folks of this city.

The discrepancies of age, in married people, is most unnatural and disgusting; whilst the merchants were at Morocco, a little girl of nine years of age was married to a man upwards of fifty. Ten and eleven is a common age for girls to be married. Much has been said of the reverence of children for their parents in the East, and tribes of people migrating therefrom, and the fifth commandment embodies the sentiment of the Eastern world. But there is little of this in Mogador; a European Jewess, who knows all the respectable Jewish and many of the Moorish families, assured me that children make their aged parents work for them, as long as the poor creatures can. "Honour thy father and thy mother, is quite as much neglected here as in Europe. However, there is some difference. The indigent Moors and Jews maintain their aged parents in their own homes, and we English Christian shut up ours in the Union Bastiles.

To continue this domestic picture, the marriage settlements, especially among the Jews, are ticklish and brittle things, as to money or other mercenary arrangements.

A match is often broken off, because a lamp of the value of four dollars has been substituted for one of the value of twenty dollars, which was first promised on the happy day of betrothal.

Indeed, nearly all marriages here are matters of sale and barter. Love is out of the question, he never flutters his purple wings over the bridal bed of Mogador. A Jewish or Moorish girl having placed before her a rich, old ugly man, of mean and villanous character, of three score years and upwards, and by his side, a handsome youth of blameless character and amiable manners, will not hesitate a moment to prefer the former. As affairs of intrigue and simple animal enjoyment are the great business of life, the ways and means, in spite of Moorish and Mahometan jealousy, as strong as death, by which these young and frail beauties indulge in forbidden conversations, are innumerable. Although the Moors frequently relate romantic legends of lovely innocent brides, who had never seen any other than the faces of their father, or of married ladies, who never raised the veil from off their faces, except to receive their own husbands, and seem to extol such chastity and seclusion; they are too frequently found indulging in obscene imaginations, tempting and seducing the weaker sex from the path of virtue and honour. So that, if women are unchaste here, or elsewhere, men are the more to blame: if woman goes one step wrong, men drag her two more. Men corrupt women, and then punish her for being corrupt, depriving them of their natural and unalienable rights.

Salt in Africa as in Europe is a domestic superstition. A Jewess, one morning, in bidding adieu to her friends, put her fingers into a salt-cellar, and took from it a large pinch of salt, which her friend told me afterwards was to preserve her from the evil one. Salt is also used for a similar important purpose, when, during the night, a person is obliged to pass from one room into another in the dark. It would be an entertaining task to collect the manifold superstitions in different parts of the world, respecting this essential ingredient of human food.

The habit of drinking white brandy, stimulates the immorality of this Maroquine society. The Jews are the great factors of this *acqua ar-*

*diente*, its Spanish and general name. Government frequently severely punishes them for making it; but they still persevere in producing this incentive to intoxication and crime. In all parts of the world, the most degraded classes are the factors of the means of vice for the higher orders of society. Moors drink it under protest, that it is not the juice of the grape. On the Sabbath, the Jewish families are all flushed, excited, and tormented by this evil spirit; but when the highest enjoyments of intellect are denied to men, they must and will seek the lower and beastly gratifications.

Friend Cohen came in one afternoon, and related several anecdotes of the Maroquine Court. When Dr. Brown was attending the Sultan, the Vizier managed to get hold of his cocked hat, and placing it upon his head, strutted about in the royal gardens. Whilst performing this feat before several attendants, the Sultan suddenly made his appearance in the midst of them. The minister seeing him, fell down in a fright and a fit. His Imperial Highness beckoned to the minister in such woful plight, to pacify himself, and put his cloak before his mouth to prevent any one from seeing him laugh at the minister, which he did most immoderately.

Cohen, who is a quack, was once consulted on a case of the harem. Cohen pleaded ignorance, God had not given him the wit; he could do nothing for the patient of his Imperial Highness. This was very politic of Cohen, for another quack, a Moor, had just been consulted, and had had his head taken off, for not being successful in the remedies he prescribed. There would not be quite so much medicine administered among us, weak, cracky, crazy mortals, in this cold damp clime, if such an alternative was proposed to our practitioners.

## CHAPTER II.

The Maroquine dynasties.—Family of the Shereefian Monarchs.—Personal appearances and character of Muley Abd Errahman.—Refutation of the charge of human sacrifices against the Moorish Princes.—Genealogy of the reigning dynasty of Morocco.—The tyrant Yezeed, (half Irish).—Muley Suleiman, the "The Shereeff of Shereefs."—Diplomatic relations of the Emperor of Morocco with European Powers.—Muley Ismael enamoured with the French Princess de Conti.—Rival diplomacy of France and England near the Maroquine Court.—Mr. Hay's correspondence with this Court on the Slave-trade.—Treaties between Great Britain and Morocco; how defective and requiring amendment.—Unwritten engagements.

Morocco, an immense and unwieldly remnant of the monarchies formed by the Saracens, or first Arabian conquerors of Africa, has had a series of dynasties terminating in that of the Shereefs.

1st. The Edristees (pure Saracens,) their capital was Fez, founded by their great progenitor, Edrio. The dynasty began in A.D. 789, and continued to 908.

2nd. The Fatamites (also Saracens.) These conquered Egypt, and were the faction of or lineal descendants of the daughter of the Prophet, the beautiful pearl-like Fatima, succeeding to the above: this dynasty continued to 972.

3rd. The Zuheirites (Zeirities, or Zereids) were usurpers of the former conquerors; their dynasty terminated in 1070.

4th. Moravedi (or Marabouteen,) that is to say, Marabouts,* who rose into consequence

---

* On account of their once possessing the throne, the Shereefs have a peculiar jealousy of Marabouts, and which latter have not forgotten their once being sovereigns of Morocco. The *Moravedi* were "really a dynasty of *priests*," as the celebrated Magi, who usurped the throne of Cyrus. The Shereefs, though descended from the Prophet, are not strictly priests, or, to make the distinction perfectly clear

about 1050, and their first prince was Aberbekr Omer El Lamethounx, a native of Sous. Their dynasty terminated in 1149.

5th. The Almohades. These are supposed to be sprung from the Berber tribes. They conquered all North Western Morocco, and reigned about one hundred years, the dynasty terminated in 1269.

6th. The Merinites. These in 1250 subjugated the kingdoms of Fez and Morocco; and in 1480 their dynasty terminated with the Shereef.

the Shereefs are to be considered a dynasty corresponding to the type of Melchizdek, uniting in themselves the regal and sacerdotal authority, whilst the *Marabouteen* were a family of priests like the sons of Aaron. Abd-el-Kader unites in himself the princely and sacerdotal authority like the Shereefs, though not of the family of the Prophet. Mankind have always been jealous of mere theocratic government, and dynasties of priests have always been failures in the arts of governing, and the Egyptian priests, though they struggled hard, and were the most accomplished of this class of men, could not make themselves the sovereigns of Egypt.

7th. The Oatagi (or Ouatasi)* were a tribe of obscure origin. In their time, the Portuguese established themselves on the coast of Morocco; their dynasty ended in 1550.

8th. The Shereefs (Oulad Ali) of the present dynasty, whose founder was Hasein, have now occupied the Imperial throne more than three centuries. This family of Shereefs came from the neighbourhood of Medina in Arabia, and succeeded to the empire of Morocco by a series of usurpations. They are divided into two branches, the Sherfah Hoseinee, so named from the founder of the dynasty, who began to reign at Taroudant and Morocco in 1524, and over all the empire in 1550, and the Sherfah El Fileli, or Tafilett, whose ancestor was Muley Shereef Ben Ali-el-Hoseinee, and assumed sovereign power at Tafilett in 1648, from which country he extended his authority over all the provinces of that empire. Thus the Shereefs began their

* According to others, the Sâdia reigned before the Shereefs.

reign in the middle of the seventeenth century, and have now wielded the sword of the Prophet as Caliph of the West these last two hundred years. I have not heard that there is anywhere a dynasty of Shereefs except in this country. They are, therefore, profoundly venerated by all true Mussulmen. It was a great error to suppose that Abd-el-Kader could have succeeded in dethroning the Emperor during the hostilities of the Emir against the lineal representative of the Prophet. Abd-el-Kader is a marabout warrior, greatly revered and idolized by all enthusiastic Mussulmen throughout North Africa, more especially in Morocco, the *terre classique* of holy-fighting men; but though the Maroquines were disaffected, groaning under the avarice of their Shereefian Lord, and occasionally do revolt, nevertheless they would not deliberately set aside the dynasty of the Shereefs, the veritable root and branch of the Prophet of God, for an adventurer of other blood, however powerful in arms and in sanctity.

Morocco is the only independent Mussulman kingdom remaining, founded by the Saracens when they conquered North Africa. Tunis and Tripoli are regencies of the Port of Tunis, having an hereditary Bey, while Tripoli is a simple Pasha, removable at pleasure. Algeria has now become an integral portion of France by the Republic.

Muley Abd Errahman was nominated to the throne by the solemn and dying request of his uncle, Muley Suleiman, to the detriment of his own children.

He belonged to one of the most illustrious branches of the reigning dynasty. In the natural order of succession, he ought to have taken possession of the Shereefian crown at the end of the last age; but, being a child, his uncle was preferred; for Mahometan sovereigns and empire are exposed to convulsions enough, without the additional dangers and elements of strife attendant on regencies.

In transmitting the sceptre to him, Muley

Suleiman, therefore, only performed an act of justice.

Muley Abd Errahman, during his long reign, rendered the imperial authority more solid than formerly, and established a species of conservative government in a semi-barbarous country, and exposed to continual commotions, like all Asiatic and African states. In governing the multitudinous and heterogeneous tribes of his empire, his grand maxim has ever been, like Austria, with her various states and hostile interests of different people, " Divide et empera." When will sovereigns learn to govern their people upon principles of homogenity of interests, natural good will, and fraternal feeling? Alas! we have reason to fear, never. It seems nations are to be governed always by setting up one portion of the people against the other.

Muley Abd Errahman was chosen by his uncle, on account of his pacific and frugal habits, educated as he was by being made in early life the administrator of the customs in Mogador, and as a prince likely to preserve and consolidate the empire. The anticipations of the uncle have been abundantly realized by the nephew, for Muley Abd Errahman, with the exception of the short period of the French hostilities, (which was not his own work and happened in spite of him), has preserved the intact without, and quiet during the many years he has occupied the throne.

His Moorish Majesty, who is advanced in life, is a man of middle stature. He has dark and expressive eyes, and, as already observed, is a mulatto of a fifth caste. Colour excites no prejudices either in the sovereign or in the subject. This Emperor is so simple in his habits and dress, that he can only be distinguished from his officers and governors of provinces by the *thall*, or parasol, the Shereefian emblem of royalty. The Emperor's son, when out on a military expedition, is also honoured by the presence of the Imperial parasol, which was found in Sidi Mohammed's tent at the Battle of Isly. Muley Abd Errahman is not given to excesses of any kind, (unless avarice is so considered), though his three harems of Fas, Miknas, and Morocco may be *stocked*, or more politely, adorned, with a thousand ladies or so, and the treasures of the empire are at his disposal. He is not a man of blood ;* he rarely decapitates a minister

* I was greatly astonished to read in Mr. Hay's "Western Barbary," (p. 123), these words—"During one of the late rebellions, a beautiful young girl was offered up as a propitiatory sacrifice, her throat being cut before the tent of the Sultan, and in his presence!" This is an unmitigated libel on the Shereefian prince ruling Morocco. First of all, the sacrifice of human beings is repudiated by every class of inhabitants in Barbary. Such rites, indeed, are unheard of, nay, unthought of. If the Mahometan religion has been powerful in any one thing, it is in that of rooting out from the mind of man every notion of human sacrifice. It is this which makes the sacrifice of the Saviour such an obnoxious doctrine to Mussulmen. It is true enough, at times, oxen are immolated to God, but not to Moorish princes, "to appease an offended potentate." One spring, when there was a great drought, the people led up to the hill of Ghamart, near Carthage, a red heifer to be slaughtered, in order to appease

or a governor, notwithstanding that he frequently confiscates their property, and sometimes imprisons them to discover their treasures, and drain them of their last farthing. The Emperor lives on good terms with the rest of his family.

the displeasure of Deity; and when the Bey's frigate, which, a short time ago, carried a present to her Britannic Majesty, from Tunis to Malta, put back by stress of weather, two sheep were sacrificed to some tutelar saints, and two guns were fired in their honour. The companions of Abd-el-Kader in a storm, during his passage from Oran to Toulon, threw handsful of salt to the raging deep to appease its wild fury. But as to sacrificing human victims, either to an incensed Deity, or to man, impiously putting himself in the place of God, the Moors of Barbary have not the least conception of such an enormity.

It would seem, unfortunately, that the practice of the gentleman, who travelled a few miles into the interior of Morocco on a horse-mission, had been to exaggerate everything, and, where effect was wanting, not to have scrupled to have recourse to unadulterated invention. But this style of writing cannot be defended on any principle, when so serious a case is brought forward as that of sacrificing a human victim to appease the wrath of an incensed sovereign, and that prince now living in amicable relations with ourselves.

He has one son, Governor of Fez (Sidi Mohammed), and another son, Governor of Rabat. The greater part of the royal family reside at Tafilett, the ancient country of the *Sherfah*, or Shereefs, and is still especially appropriated for their residence. Ali Bey reported as the information of his time, that there were at Tafilett no less than two thousand Shereefs, who all pretended to have a right to the throne of Morocco, and who, for that reason, enjoyed certain gratifications paid them by the reigning Sultan. He adds that, during an interregnum, many of them took up arms and threw the empire into anarchy. This state of things is happily past, and, as to the number of the Shereefs at Tafilett, all that we know is, there is a small fortified town, inhabited entirely by Shereefs, living in moderate, if not impoverished circumstances.

The Shereefian Sultans of Morocco are not only the successors of the Arabian Sovereigns of Spain, but may justly dispute the Caliphat with the Osmanlis, or Turkish Sultans. Their right to be the chiefs of Islamism is better founded than the pretended Apostolic successors at Rome, who, in matters of religion, they in some points resemble.

I introduce here, with some unimportant variations, a translation from Gräberg de Hëmso of the Imperial Shereefian pedigree, to correspond with the genealogical tableaux, which the reader will find in succeeding pages, of the Moorish dynasties of Tunis and Tripoli.

### GENEALOGY OF THE REIGNING DYNASTY OF MOROCCO.

1. Ali-Ben-Abou-Thaleb; died in 661 of the Christian Era; surnamed "The accepted of God," of the most ancient tribe of Hashem, and husband of Fatima, styled Ey-Zarah, or, "The Pearl," only daughter of Mahomet.

2. Hosein, or El-Hosein-es-Sebet, *i.e.* "The Nephew;" died in 1680; from him was de-

rived the patronymic El-Hoseinee, which all the Shereefs bear.

3. Hasan-el-Muthna, *i.e.* "The Striker;" died in 719; brother of Mohammed, from whom pretended to descend, in the 16th degree, Mohammed Ben Tumert, founder of the dynasty of the Almohadi, in 1120.

4. Abdullah-el-Kamel, *i.e.* "The Perfect;" in 752, father of Edris, the progenitor or founder of the dynasty of the Edristi in Morocco, and who had six brothers.

5. Mohammed, surnamed "The pious and just soul;" in 784, had five children who were the branches of a numerous family. (Between Mohammed and El-Hasem who follows, some assert that three gererations succeeded).

6. El-Kasem, in 852; brother of Abdullah, from whom it is said the Caliphs of Egypt and Morocco are descended.

7. Ismail; about 890.

8. Ahmed; in 901.

9. El-Hasan; in 943.

10. Ali; in 970, (excluded from the genealogy published by Ali Bey, but noted by several good authorities).

11. Abubekr; 996.

12. El-Husan, in 1012.

13. Abubekr El-Arfat, *i.e.* "The Knower," in 1043.

14. Mohammed, in 1071.

15. Abdullah, in 1109.

16. Hasan, in 1132; brother of a Mohammed, who emigrated to Morocco.

17. Mohammed, in 1174.

18. Abou-el-Kasem Abd Errahman, in 1207.

19. Mohammed, in 1236.

20. El-Kasem, in 1271, brother of Ahmed, who also emigrated into Africa, and was father of eight children, one of whom was:

21. El-Hasan, who, in 1266, upon the demand of a tribe of Berbers of Moghrawa, was sent by his father into the kingdom of Segelmesa (now Tafilett) and Draha, where,

through his descendants, he became the common progenitor of the Maroquine Shereefs.

22. Mohammed, in 1367.

23. El-Hasan, in 1391, by his son, Mohammed, he became grandfather of Hosem, who, during 1507, founded the first dynasty of the Hoseinee Shereefs in Segelmesa, and the extreme south of Morocco, which dynasty, after twelve years, made itself master of the kingdom of Morocco.

24. Ali-es-Shereef, *i.e.* "The noble," died in 1437, was the first to assume this name, and had, after forty years elapsed, two sons, the first, Muley Mahommed, by a concubine, and the second:

25. Yousef, by a legitimate wife; he retired into Arabia, where he died in 1485. It was said of Yousef, that no child was born to him until his eightieth year, when he had five children, the first born of which was,

26. Ali, who died in 1527, and had at least, eighty male children.

27. Mohammed, in 1691, brother of Muley Meherrez, a famous brigand, and afterwards a king of Tafilett: this Mohammed was father of many children, and among the rest—

28. Ali, who was called by his uncle from Zambo (?) into Moghrele-el-Aksa Morocco about the year 1620, and died in 1632, after having founded the second, and present, dynasty of the Hoseinee Shereefs, surnamed the *Filei*.

Muley Shereeff, died in 1652; he had eighty sons, and a hundred and twenty-four daughters.

30. Muley Ismail, in 1727.
31. Muley Abdullah, in 1757.
32. Sidi Mohammed, in 1789.
33. Muley Yezeed, who assumed the surname of El-Mahdee *i. e.* "the director," in 1792.
34. Muley Hisham, in 1794.
35. Muley Suleiman, in 1822.
36. Muley Abd Errahman, nephew of

Muley Suleiman and eldest son of Muley Hisham, the reigning Shereefian prince.*

In the Shereefian lineage of Muley Suleiman, copied for Ali Bey by the Emperor himself, and which is very meagre and unsatisfactory, we miss the names of the two brothers, the Princes Yezeed and Hisham, who disputed the succession on the death of their father, Sidi Mohammed which happened in April 1790 or 1789, when the Emperor was on a military expedition to quell the rebellion of his son, Yezeed—the tyrant whose bad fame and detestable cruelties

* Gräberg de Hemso, whilst consul-general for Sweden and Sardinia (at Morocco!) concludes the genealogy of these Mussulman sovereigns with this strange, but Catholic-spirited rhapsody:—

"Muley Abd-ur-Bakhman, who is now gloriously and happily reigning, whom we pray Almighty God, all Goodness and Power, to protect and exalt by prolonging his life, glory, and reign in this world and in the next; and giving him, during eternity, the heavenly beatitude, in order that his soul, in the same manner as flame to flame, river to sea, may be united with his sweetest, most perfect and ineffable Creator. Amen."

filled with horror all the North African world. The Emperor Suleiman evidently suppressed these names, as disfiguring the lustre of the holy pedigree; although Yezeed was the hereditary prince, and succeeded his father three days after his death, being proclaimed Sultan at Salee with accustomed pomp and magnificence. This monster in human shape, having excited a civil war against himself by his horrid barbarities, was mortally wounded by a poisoned arrow, shot from a secret hand, and died in February 1792, the 22nd month of his reign, and 44th year of his age.

On being struck with the fatal weapon, he was carried to his palace at Dar-el-Beida, where he only survived a single day; but yet during this brief period, and whilst in the agony of dissolution, it is said, the tyrant committed more crimes and outrages, and caused more people to be sacrificed, than in his whole lifetime, determining with the vengeance of a pure fiend, that if his people would not weep for his death they should mourn for the loss of their friends and relations, like the old tyrant Herod. How instinctively imitative is crime! Yezeed was of course, not buried at the cross-roads, (Heaven forefend!) or in a cemetery for criminals and infidels, for being a Shereef, and divine (not royal) blood running in his veins, he was interred with great solemnities at the mosque of *Kobah Sherfah* (tombs of the Shereefs), beside the mausoleums wherein repose the awful ashes of the princes and kings, who, in ages gone by, have devastated the Empire of Morocco, and inflicted incalculable miseries on its unfortunate inhabitants, whilst plenarily exercising their divine right, to do wrong as sovereigns, or as invested with inviolable Shereefian privileges as lineal successors of the Prophets of God!*

* Yezeed was half-Irish, born of the renegade widow of an Irish sergeant of the corps of Sappers and Miners, who was placed at the disposition of this government by England, and who died in Morocco. On his death, the facile, buxom

A civil war still followed this monster's death, and the empire was rent and partitioned

widow was admitted, "nothing loath," into the harem of Sidi-Mohammed, who boasted of having within its sacred enclosure of love and bliss, a woman from every clime.

Here the daughter of Erin brought forth this ferocious tyrant, whose maxim of carnage, and of inflicting suffering on humanity was, "My empire can never be well governed, unless a stream of blood flows from the gate of the palace to the gate of the city." To do Yezeed justice, he followed out the instincts of his birth, and made war on all the world except the English (or Irish). Tully's Letters on Tripoli give a graphic account of the exploits of Yezeed, who, to his inherent cruelty, added a fondness for practical (Hibernian) jokes.

His father sent him several times on a pilgrimage to Mecca to expiate his crimes, when he amused, or alarmed, all the people whose countries he passed through, by his terrific vagaries. One day he would cut off the heads of a couple of his domestics, and play at bowls with them; another day, he would ride across the path of an European, or a consul, and singe his whiskers with the discharge of a pistol-shot; another day, he would collect all the poor of a district, and gorge them with a razzia he had made on the effects of some rich over-fed Bashaw. The multitude sometimes implored heaven's blessing on the head of Yezeed, at other times trem-

into three portions, in each of which a pretender disputed for the possession of the Shereefian throne. The poor people had now three tyrants for one. The two grand competitors, however, were Muley Hisham, who was proclaimed Sultan in the south at Morrocco and Sous, and Muley Suleiman, who was saluted as Emperor in the north at Fez. In 1795, Hisham retired to a sanctuary where he soon died, and then Muley Suleiman was proclaimed in the southern provinces Emir-el-Monmeneen, and Sultan of the whole empire.

Muley Suleiman proved to be a good and patriotic prince, " the Shereef of Shereefs," whilst he maintained, by a just administration, tranquility in his own state, and cultivated peace with Europe. During his long reign of a quar-

bled for their own heads. Meanwhile, our European consuls made profound obeisance to this son of the Shereef, enthroned in the West. So the tyrant passed the innocent days of his pilgrimage. So the godless herd of mankind acquiesced in the divine rights of royalty.

ter of a century, at a period when all the christian powers were convulsed with war, he wisely remained neutral, and his subjects were happy in the enjoyment of peace and prosperity. He died on the 28th March 1820, about the 50th year of his age, after having, with his last breath declared his nephew, Muley Abd Errahman, the legitimate and hereditary successor of the Shereefs, and so restoring the lineal descent of these celebrated Mussulman sovereigns. The most glorious as well as the most beneficent and acceptable act of the reign of Muley Suleiman, so far as European nations were concerned, was the abolition of christian slavery in his States. In former times, the Maroquine Moors, smarting under the ills inflicted upon them by Spain and breathing revenge, subjected their Christian captives to more cruel bondage, than ever were experienced by the same victims of the Corsairs in Algeria, the stronghold of this nefarious trade.

The Shereefs have been accustomed to wrap

themselves up in their sublime indifference, as to the fate and fortunes of Europe. During late centuries, their diplomatic intercourse with European princes has been scarcely relieved by a single interesting event, beyond their piratical wars and our complaisant redemptions of their prisoners. But, in the reign of Louis XIV., Muley Ismail having heard an extremely seductive account of the Princesse de Conti (Mademoiselle de Blois), natural daughter of the Grand Monarch and Mademoiselle de la Vallière, by means of his ambassador, Abdullah Ben Aissa, had the chivalrous temerity to demand her in marriage. "Our Sultan," said the ambassador, "will marry her according to the law of God and the Prophet, but she shall not be forced to abandon her religion, or manner of living; and she will be able to find all that her heart desires in the palace of my sovereign—if it please God."

This request, of course, could not be granted, but the "king of Christian kings" replied very graciously," that the difference alone of religion prevented the consummation of the happiness of the Shereef of Shereefs." This humble demand of the hand of the princess mightily amused " the Court of Courts," and its hireling poets taxed their wit to the utmost in chanting the praises of the royal virgin, who had attacked the regards (or the growls) of the Numidian Tiger, as Muley Ismail was politely designated. Take this as a specimen.—

> " Votre beauté, grande princesse,
>   Porte les traits dont elle blesse
>   Jusques aux plus sauvages lieux :
>   L'Afrique avec vous capitule,
>   Et les conquêtes de vos yeux
>   Vont plus loin que celles d'Hercule."

The Maroquine ambassador, who was also grand admiral of the Moorish navy, witnessing all the wonders of Paris at the epoch of the Great Monarch, was dazzled with its beauty and magnificence; nevertheless, he remained a good Mussulman. He was besides a grateful man, for he saw our James II. in exile, who had given the admiral liberty without ransom when he had been captured by English cruisers, and heartily thanked the fallen prince for his own freedom whilst he condoled with him in his misfortunes. But the Moorish envoy, in spite of his great influence, was unable to conclude the treaty of peace, which was desired by France. On his return to Morocco, the ambassador had so advanced in European ideas of convenience, or civilization, that he attempted to introduce a taste for Parisian luxury among his own countrymen.

As in many other parts of the Mediterranean, France and England have incessantly contended for influence at the Court of Morocco. Various irregular missions to this Court have been undertaken by European powers, from the first establishment of the Moorish empire of the West. The French entered regularly into relations with the western Moors shortly after us;

their flag, indeed, began to appear at their ports in 1555, under Francis I. They succeeded in gaining the favour of the Moors whilst we occupied Tangier, and Louis XIV encouraged them in their efforts to attack or harass our garrison. The nature of our struggles with the Moors of Morocco can be at once conjectured from the titles of the pamphlets published in those times, viz.

" *Great* and *bloody* news of Tangier," (London 1680), and " The Moors *blasted*, being a discourse concerning Tangier, especially when it was under the Earl of Teviot," (London, 1681). But, after the peace of Utrecht, conceding Gibraltar to England, and which more than compensated us for the loss of Tangier, the influence of France in Morocco began to wane, and the trade of this empire was absorbed by the British during the 18th century. Then, in the beginning of our own age, the battle of Trafalgar, and the fall of Napoleon, established the supremacy of British influence over the minds of the

Shereefs, which has not been yet entirely effaced.

Our diplomatic intercouse has been more frequent and interesting with the Western Moors since the French occupation of Algeria, and we have exerted our utmost to neutralize the spirit of the war party in Fez, seconding the naturally pacific mind of Muley Abd Errahman, in order to remove every pretext of the French for invading this country. How we succeeded in a critical period will be mentioned at the close of the present work.\* But this port, and our influence receiving thereby a great shock, I am happy to state that the latest account from this most interesting Moorish country, represents Muley Abd Errahman as steadily pursuing, by the assistance of his new vizier, Bouseilam, the most pacific policy. This minister, being very rich, is enabled to consolidate his power by frequent presents to his royal master, thus gratifying the most darling passion of Muley Abd Errah-

\* See Appendix at the end of this volume.

man, and Vizier and Sultan amuse themselves by undertaking plundering expeditions against insurrectionary tribes, whose sedition they first stimulate, and then quell, that is to say, by receiving from the unlucky rebels a handsome gratification.

The late Mr. Hay entered into a correspondence with the Shereefian Court for the purpose of drawing its attention to the subject of the slave-trade, and I shall make an extract or two from the letters, bearing as they do on my present mission.

From three letters addressed by the Sultan to Mr. Hay, I extract the following passages. "Be it known to you, that the traffic in slaves is a matter on which all sects and nations have agreed from the time of the sons of Adam, (on whom be the peace of God up to this day). And we are not yet aware of its being prohibited by the laws of any sect, and no one need ask this question, the same being manifest to both high and low, and requires no more demonstration than the light of the day."

The Apostle of God is quoted as enforcing upon the master to give his slave the same clothing as himself, and not to exact more labour from him than he can perform.

Another letter. " It has been prohibited to sell a Muslem, the sacred *misshaf*, and a young person to an unbeliever, that is to any one who does not profess the faith of Islam, whether Christian, Jew, or Majousy. To make a present, or to give as in alms is held in the same light as a sale. The said Sheikh Khalil also says, " a slave is emancipated by the law if ill-treated, that is, whether he intends or does actually ill-treat him. But whether a slave can take with him what he possesses of property or no, is a matter yet undecided by the doctors of the law."

Another. " Be it known to you, that the religion of Islam—may God exalt it! has a solid foundation, of which the corner stones are well secured, and the perfection whereof has been made known to us by God, to whom belongs all praise in his book, the Forkam (or Koran, (which admits neither of addition nor diminution. As regards the making of slaves and trading therewith, it is confirmed by our book, as also of the *Sunnat* (or traditions) of our Prophet. There is no controversy among the *Oulamma* (doctors) on the subject. No one can allow what is prohibited or prohibit that which is lawful."

These extracts shew the *animus* of the Shereefian correspondence. To attack the Shereefs on this point of slavery, is to besiege the citadel of their religion, or that is the interpretation which they are pleased to put upon the matter; but all forms of bigotry and false principles will ultimately succumb to the force of truth.

It is necessary to persevere, to persevere always, and the end will be obtained.

I shall add a word or two on our treaties, or capitulations, as they are disgracefully called, with the Empire of Morocco, intimating, as they do, our former submission to the arrogant, piratical demands of the Barbary Powers in the days of their corsair glory. Our political relations with Morocco officially commenced in the times of Elizabeth, or Charles I; but the formal treaty of peace was not concluded until the last year of the reign of George 1, which was ratified in 1729 by George II, and by the Sultan Muley Ahmed-elt-Thabceby "The golden." Then followed various other treaties for the security of persons and trade, and against piracy. All, however, of any value, are embodied in the treaty between Great Britain and Morocco, signed at Fez, 14th June 1801, and confirmed, 19th January 1824 by the Sultan Muley Suleiman, which is considered as still in force, and from which I shall extract two or three articles, appending observations, for the purpose of shewing its spirit and bearing on European commerce and civilization. Common sense tells us that trade can only flourish where there is security for life and property. We have to examine, whether this security is fully guaranteed to British subjects, residing in and trading with the empire to Morocco, by the treaty of 1801 and 1824.

This treaty begins with consuls, and sufficiently provides for their honour and safety. It then states the privilege of British subjects, and more particulary of merchants, residing in, and wishing to engage in commercial speculations in Morocco. These privileges are, on the whole, also explicitly stated. Afterwards follows two articles on "disputes," which clauses were amended and explained in January 1824, when the treaty was confirmed. These are:—

"VII. Disputes between Moorish subjects and English subjects, shall be decided in the presence of the English Consuls, provided the decision be comformable to the Moorish law, in which case the English subject shall not go before the Kady or Hakem, as the Consul's decision shall suffice.

"VIII. Should any dispute occur between English subjects and Moors, and that dispute should occasion a complaint from either of the parties, the Emperor of Morocco shall only decide the matter. If the English subject be guilty, he shall not be punished with more severity than a Moor would be; should he escape, no other subject of the English nation shall be arrested in his stead, and if the escape be made after the decision, in order to avoid punishment, he shall be sentenced as a Moor would be who had committed the same crime. Should any dispute occur in the English territories, between a Moor and an English subject, it shall be decided by an equal number of the Moors residing there and of Christians, according to the custom of the place, if not contrary to the Moorish law."

In the amended clause of Article VIII. We have for any complaint, substituted serious personal injury, and I cannot but observe that the making of the Emperor the final judge, in such case, is a stretch of too great confidence in Moorish justice.

Not that a Sultan of Morocco is necessarily bad or worse than an European Sovereign, but because a personage of such power and character, armed with unbounded attributes of despotism over his own subjects, who are considered his Abeed, or slaves, whilst feebly aided by the perception of the common rights of men, and imperfectly acquainted with Europcen civilization, can never, unless, indeed by accident or miracle, justly decide upon the case of an Englishman, or upon a dispute between his own and a foreign subject; for besides the ideas and education of the Emperor, there is the necessity which his Imperial Highness feels, despot as he is, of exhibiting himself before his people as their undoubted friend and partial judge.

So strongly have Sultans of Morocco felt

this, that many anecdotes might be cited where the Emperor has indemnified the foreigner for injury done to him by his own subjects, whilst he has represented to them that he has decided the case against the stranger. It is surprising how a British Government could surrender the settlement of the dispute of their subjects to the final appeal of the Court of Morocco in the nineteenth century, and, moreover, allow them to be decided, according to the maxims of the Mohammedan code, or comformable to the Moorish law! It is not long ago since, indeed just before my arrival in Morocco, that the Emperor decided a dispute in rather a summary manner, without even the usual Moorish forms of judicial proceedure by decapitating, a quasi—European Jew, under French protection, and who once acted as the Consul of France.

There is something singularly deficient and wrong, although to persons unacquainted with Barbary, it looks sufficiently fair and just, in the provision—" he (the English guilty subject) shall not be punished with more severity than a Moor could be," fairly made? In the first place, although this does not come under the idea of " serious personal injury," would the English people approve of their countrymen suffering the same punishment as the Moors for theft, by cutting off their right hand? Moors and Arabs have been so maimed for life, on being convicted of stealing property to the value of a single shilling! Who will take upon himself to enumerate the punishments, which may be, and are inflicted for grave offences? It may be replied that this stipulation of punishing British subjects, like Moorish, is only on paper, and we have no examples of its being put into execution. I rejoin, without attempting to cite proof, that, whilst such an article exists in a treaty, said to be binding on the Government of England as well as Morocco, there can be no real security for British subjects in this country; for in the event of the Maroquines acting strictly upon the articles of this treaty, what mode of inculpation, or what colour of right, can the British Government adopt or shew against them? and what are treaties made for, if they do not bind both parties?

In illustration of the way in which British subjects have their disputes sometimes settled, according to Articles VII and VIII, I take the liberty of introducing the case of Mr. Saferty, a respectable Gibraltar merchant, settled at Mogador. A few months before my arrival in that place, this gentleman was adjudged, in the presence of his Consul, Mr. Willshire, and the Governor of Mogador, for repelling an insult offered to him by a Moor, and sentenced to be imprisoned with felons and cut-throats in a horrible dungeon. However, Mr. Saferty was attended by a numerous body of his friends; so when the sentence was given, a cry of indignation arose, a scuffle ensued, and the prisoner was rescued from the Moorish police-officers. Mr. Willshire found the means of patching up the business with the Moorish authorities, and the case was soon forgotten. " All's well that ends well."

I do not say that the Moors are determinedly vindictive, or seek quarrels with Europeans; on the contrary, I believe the cause of the dispute frequently rests with the European, and the bonâ-fide agressor, some adventurer whose conduct was so bad in his own country, that he sought Barbary as a refuge from the pursuit of the minister of justice. What I wish to lay stress on is, the enormous power given to the Emperor, by a solemn treaty, in making him the final judge, and the imminent exposure of British subjects to the barbarous punishments of a semi-civilized people.

Article X is a most singular one. " Renegades from the English nation, or subjects who change their religion to embrace the Moorish, they being of unsound mind at the time of turning Moors, shall not be admitted as Moors, and may again return to their former religion;

but if they afterwards resolve to be Moors, they must abide by their own decision, and their excuses will not be accepted."

It was a wonderful discovery of our modern morale, that a renegade, being a madman, should not be considered a renegade in earnest, or responsible for his actions. Nevertheless, these unfortunate beings, should they have better thoughts, or as mad-doctors have it, " a lucid interval," and leave the profession of the Mahometan faith, and afterwards again relapse into madness, and turn Mahometans once more, are doomed to irretrievable slavery, or if they relapse, to death itself; the Mahometan law, punishes relapsing renegades with death. This curious clause says, "that though being madmen, they must abide their decision (of unreason) and their excuses will not be accepted." This said article was confirmed as late as the year 1824 by the plenipotentiary of a nation, which boasts of being the most free and civilized of Europe, and whose people spend annually millions for the conversion of the heathen, and the extinction of the slave-trade.

The last clause of Article IV also demands our attention, viz. "And if any English merchant should happen to have a vessel in or outside the port, he may go on board himself, or any of his people, without being liable to pay anything whatever."

Now in spite of this (but of course forgotten) stipulation, the merchants of Mogador are not permitted to visit their own vessels, nor those of other persons which may happen to be in or outside the port. It is true, the authorities plead the reason of their refusal to be, "The merchants are indebted to the Emperor:" neither will the authorities take any security, and arbitrarily, and insolently prohibit, under any circumstances, the merchants from visiting their vessels. I have said enough to shew that our treaties (I beg the reader's pardon, " capitulations") with the Emperor of Morocco, require immediate revision, and to be amended with articles more suited to the spirit of the age, and European civilization, as likewise more consistent with the dignity of Great Britian.

The treaty for the supply of provisions, especially cattle, to the garrison of Gibraltar is either a verbal one, or a secret arrangement, for no mention is made of it in the published state paper documents. It is probably a mere verbal unwritten understanding, but, nevertheless, is more potent in its working than the written treaties. This is not the first time that the unwritten has proved stronger than the written engagement.

## CHAPTER III.

The two different aspects by which the strength and resources of the Empire of Morocco may be viewed or estimated.—Native appellation of Morocco.—Geographical limits of this country.—Historical review of the inhabitants of North Africa, and the manner in which this region was successively peopled and conquered.—The distinct varieties of the human race, as found in Morocco.—Nature of the soil and climate of this country.—Derem, or the Atlas chain of mountains.—Natural products.—The Shebbel, or Barbary salmon; different characters of exports of the Northern and Southern provinces.—The Elæonderron Argan.—Various trees and plants.—Mines.—The Sherb-Errech, or Desert-horse.

The empire of Morocco may be considered under two aspects, as to its extent, and as to its influence. It may be greatly circumscribed or expanded to an almost indefinite extent, according to the feelings, or imagination, of the writer, or speaker. A resident here gave me a meagre *tableau*, something like this,

| | | |
|---|---|---|
| The city of Morocco. | . | 50,000 souls. |
| ,,  Fez. | . . | 40,000 ,, |
| ,,  Mequinez. | . | 25,000 ,, |
| | | 115,000 ,, |

The maritime cities contain little more than 100,000 inhabitants, making altogether about 220,000. Over the provinces of the south, Sous and Wadnoun, the Sultan has no real power; so the south is cut off as an integral portion of the empire. Over the Rif, or the northern Berber provinces, the Sultan exercises a precarious sovereignty, every man's gun or knife is there his law and authority. Fez contains a disaffected population, teeming some years since with the adherents of Abd-el-Kader.

Then the Atlas is full of quasi-independent Berber tribes, who detest equally the Arabs and the Moorish government; finally, Tafilett and the provinces on the eastern side of the Atlas, are too remote to feel the influence of the central government.

As to military force, the Emperor's standing army does not amount to more than 20 or 30,000 Nigritian troops, and all cavalry. The irregular and contingent cavalry and infantry can never be depended upon, even under such a chief as Abd-el-Kader was. They must always be fed, but they will not, at any summons, leave the cultivation of their fields, or their wives and children defenceless.

As to the commerce of the Empire, with fifty ships visiting Mogador and other maritime cities, the amount, per annum, does not exceed forty millions of francs, or about a million and a half sterling including imports and exports. Such is the view of the Empire on the depreciating side.

Another resident of this country gives the opposite or more favourable view.

The Sultan is the head of the orthodox religion of the Mussulmen of the West, and more firmly established on his throne than the Sultan of the Ottomans. His influence, as a sovereign Shereef, spreads throughout Western Barbary and Central Africa, wherever there is a Mussulman to be found. In the event of an enemy appearing in the shape of a Christian, or Infidel, all would unite, including the most disjointed and hostile tribes against the common foe of Islamism.

The Sultan, upon an emergency or insurrection in his own empire, by the politic distribution of titles of *Marabout* (often used as a species of degree of D.D.) and other honours attached to the Shereefian Parasol, can likewise easily excite one chief against another, and consolidate his power over their intestine divisions. His Moorish Majesty, at any rate, has always actual possession in his favour; and, whether he really governs the whole Empire or not, or to the extent which he has presumed to mark out its boundaries, he can always proclaim to his disjointed provinces that he does so govern it and exercise authority; and, in general, he does succeed in making both his own people and foreign nations believe in his pretensions, and acknowledge his power.

The truth lies, perhaps, between these extremes. The Shereefs once pretended to exercise authority over all Western Sahara as far as Timbuctoo, that is to say, all that region of the great desert lying west of the Touaricks.

The account of the expedition of the Shereef Mohammed, who penetrated as far as Wadnoun, and which took place more than three centuries ago, as related by Marmol, leaves no doubt of the ancient ambition of the sovereign of Morocco. And although this pretension has now been given up, they still claim sovereignty over the oases of Touat, a month's journey in the Sahara. Formerly, indeed, the authority of the Maroquine

Sultans over Touat and the south appears to have been more real and effective.

Diego de Torres relates that, in his time, the Shereefs maintained a force of ten thousand cavalry in the provinces of Draha, Tafilett and Jaguriri, and Monsieur Mouette counts Touat as one of the provinces of the Empire. The Sheikh Haj Kasem, in the itinerary which he dictated to Monsieur Delaporte, says that, about forty years ago, Agobli and Taoudeni depended on Morocco. This, however, is what the people of Ghadames told me, whilst they admitted that the oases neither did contain a single officer of the Emperor, nor did the people pay his Shereefian Highness the smallest impost. The Sultan's authority is now indeed purely nominal, and the French look forward to the time when these fine and centrally placed oases will form " une dépendance de l'Algérie."

The only countries in the South which now pay a regular impost to the Emperor, are Tafilett, limited to the valley of Fez, Wad-

Draha as far as the lake Ed-Debaia, and Sous. The countries of Sidi, Hashem, and Wadnoun nominally acknowledge the Emperor, and occasionally send a present; but the most mountainous, between Sous and Wad-Draha, which has been called Guezoula or Gouzoula, and is said to be peopled by a Berber race, sprang from the ancient Gelulir, is entirely independent. In the north and west are also many quasi-independent tribes, but still the Emperor keeps up a sort of authority over them; and, if nothing more, is content simply with being called *their* Sultan.

Maroquine Moors call their country El-Gharb, "The West," and sometimes Mogrel-el-Aska, that is "The far West:* the name seems to have originated something in the same way among the Saracenic conquerors, as the "Far West" with the Anglo-Americans, arising from an apprehensive feeling of indefinite extent of

* The middle Western Region consists of Algiers and part of Tunis.

unexplored country. Among the Moors generally, Morocco is now often called, "Blad Muley Abd Errahman, or "Country of the Sultan Muley Abd Errahman." The northwestern portion of Morocco was first conquered; Morocco Proper, Sous and Tafilett were added with the progress of conquest. But scarcely a century has elapsed since their union under one common Sultan, whilst the diverse population of the four States are solely kept together by the interests and feelings of a common religion.

The Maroquine Empire, with its present limits, is bounded on the north by the Mediterranean Sea and the Straits of Gibraltar, on the west by the Atlantic Ocean and the Canary and Madeira Islands, on the south by the deserts of Noun Draha and the Sahara, on the east by Algeria, the Atlas, and Tafilett, on the borders of Sahara beyond their eastern slopes. The greatest length from north to south is about five hundred miles, with a breadth from east to west varying considerably at an average of two hundred, containing an available or really *dependent* territory of some 137,400 square miles, or nearly as large as Spain; and the whole is situate between the 28° and 40° N. Latitude. Monsieur Benou, in his "Description Géographique de l'Empire de Maroc" says Morocco " comprend une superficie d'environ 5,775 myriamètres carrés, un peu plus grande, par conséquant, que celle de la France, qui équivaut à 5,300." This then is the available and immediate territory of Morocco, not comprising distant dependencies, where the Shereefs exercise a precarious or nominal sovereignty.

Previously to particularizing the population of Morocco, I shall take the liberty of introducing some general observations on the whole of the inhabitants of North Africa, and the manner in which this country was successively peopled and conquered. Greek and Roman classics contain only meagre and confused notions of the aborigines of North Africa, although they have left us a mass of details on the Punic wars, and the struggles which ensued between the Romans and the ancient Libyans, before the domination of the Latin Republic could be firmly established. Herodotus cites the names of a number of people who inhabited North Africa, mostly confining himself to repeat the fables or the more interesting facts, of which they were the object.

The nomenclature of Strabo is neither so extensive, nor does it contain more precise or correct information. He mentions the celebrated oasis of Ammonium and the nation of the Nasamones. Farther west, behind Carthage and the Numidians, he also notices the Getulians, and after them the Garamantes, a people who appear to have colonized both the oasis of Ghadames and the oases of Fezzan. Ptolemy makes the whole of the Mauritania, including Algeria and Morocco, to be bounded on the south by tribes, called Gætuliæ and Melanogæluti, on the south the latter evidently having contracted alliance of blood with the negroes.

According to Sallust, who supports himself upon the authority of Heimpsal, the Carthaginian historian, "North Africa was first occupied by Libyans and Getulians, who were a barbarous people, a heterogeneous mass, or agglomeration of people of different races, without any form of religion or government, nourishing themselves on herbs, or devouring the raw flesh of animals killed in the chase; for first amongst these were found Blacks, probably some from the interior of Africa, and belonging to the great negro family; then whites, issue of the Semitic stock, who apparently constituted, even at that early period, the dominant race or caste. Later, but at an epoch absolutely unknown, a new horde of Asiatics," says Sallust, " of Medes, Persians, and Armenians, invaded the countries of the Atlas, and, led on by Hercules, pushed their conquests as far as Spain."*

* Pliny, the Elder, confirms this tradition mentioned by

The Persians, mixing themselves with the former inhabitants of the coast, formed the tribes called Numides, or Numidians (which embrace the provinces of Tunis and Constantina), whilst the Medes and the Armenians, allying themselves with the Libyans, nearer to Spain, it is pretended, gave existence to a race of Moors, the term Medes being changed into that of Moors.\*

As to the Getulians confined in the valleys of the Atlas, they resisted all alliance with the new immigrants, and formed the principal nucleus of those tribes who have ever remained in North Africa, rebels to a foreign civilization, or rather determined champions of national freedom, and whom, imitating the Romans and Arabs, we are pleased to call Barbarians or Berbers (Barbari

Pliny. Marcus Varron reports, "that in all Spain there are spread Iberians, Persians, Phœnicians, Celts, and Carthaginians." (Lib. iii. chap. 2).

\* In Latin, Mauri, Maurice, Maurici, Maurusci, and it is supposed, so called by the Greeks from their dark complexions.

Brâber\*), and whence is derived the name of the Barbary States. But the Romans likewise called the aboriginal tribes of North Africa, Moors, or Mauri, and some contend that Moors and Berbers are but two different names for the aboriginal tribes, the former being of Greek and the latter of African origin. The Romans might, however, confound the African term *berber* with *barbari,* which latter they applied, like the Greeks, to all strangers and foreigners.

The revolutions of Africa cast a new tribe of emigrants upon the North African coast, who, if we are to believe the Byzantine historian,

\* The more probable derivation of this word is from *bar,* signifying land, or earth, in contradistinction from the sea, or desert, beyond the cultivable lands to the South. To give the term more force it is doubled, after the style of the Semitic reduplication. De Haedo de la Captividad gives a characteristic derivation, like a genuine hidalgo, who proclaimed eternal war against Los Moros. He says—" Moors, Alartes, Cabayles, and some Turks, form all of them a dirty, lazy, inhuman, indomitable nation of beasts, and it is for this reason that, for the last few years, I have accustomed myself to call that land the land of Barbary."

Procopius, of the sixth century, were no other than Canaanites, expelled from Palestine by the victorious arms of Joshua, when he established the Israelites in that country. Procopius affirms that, in his time, there was a column standing at Tigisis, on which was this inscription:— "We are those who fled from the robber Joshua, son of Nun."* Now whether Tigisis was in Algeria, or was modern Tangier, as some suppose, it is certain there are several traditions among the Berber tribes of Morocco, which relate that their ancestors were driven out of Palestine. Also, the Berber historian, Ebn-Khal-Doun, who flourished in the fourteenth century, makes all the Berbers descend from one Bar, the son of Mayigh, son of Canaan. However, what may be the truths of these traditions of Sallust or Procopius, there is no difficulty in believing that North Africa was peopled by fugitive and roving tribes, and that the first settlers should be exposed to be

* Procopius, de Bello Vandilico, lib. ii. cap. 10.

plundered by succeeding hordes; for such has been the history of the migrations of all the tribes of the human race.

But the most ancient historical fact on which we can depend is, the invasion, or more properly, the successive invasions of North Africa by the Phœnicians. Their definite establishment on these shores took place towards the foundation of Carthage, about 820 years before our era. Yet we know little of their intercourse or relations with the aboriginal tribes. When the Romans, a century and a half before Christ, received, or wrested, the rule of Africa from the Phœnicians, or Carthaginians, they found before them an indigenous people, whom they indifferently called Moors, Berbers, or Barbarians. A part of these people were called also Nudides, which is perhaps considered the same term as nomades.

Some ages later, the Romans, too weak to resist a vigorous invasion of other conquerors, were subjugated by the Vandals, who, during a century, held possession of North Africa; but, after this time, the Romans again raised their heads, and completely expelled or extirpated the Vandals, so that, as before, there were found only two people or races in Africa: the Romans and the Moors, or aborigines.

Towards the middle of the seventh century after Christ, and a few years after the death of Mahomet, the Romans, in the decline of their power, had to meet the shock of the victorious arms of the Arabians, who poured in upon them triumphant from the East; but, too weak to resist this new tide of invasion, they opposed to them the aborigines, which latter were soon obliged to continue alone the struggle.

The Arabian historians, who recount these wars, speak of *Roumi* or Romans (of the Byzantine empire) and the Brâber—evidently the aboriginal tribes—who promptly submitted to the Arabs to rid themselves of the yoke of the Romans; but, after the retreat of their ancient masters, they revolted and remained a long time in arms against their new conquerors—a rule of action which all subjugated nations have been wont to follow. Were we English now to attempt to expel the French from Algeria, we, undoubtedly, should be joined by the Arabs; but who would, most probably, soon also revolt against us, were we to attempt to consolidate our dominion over them.

In the first years of the eighth century, and at the end of the first century of the Hegira, the conquering Arabs passed over to Spain, and, inasmuch as they came from Mauritania, the people of Spain gave them the name of Moors (that of the aborigines of North Africa), although they had, perhaps, nothing in common with them, if we except their Asiatic origin. Another and most singular name was also given to these Arab warriors in France and other parts of Europe—that of Saracens—whose etymology is extremely obscure.* From this time

* Some derive it from *Sarak*, an Arabic word which signifies to steal, and hence, call the conquerors thieves.

the Spaniards have always given the names of Moors (*los Moros*), not only to the Arabs of Spain, but to all the Arabs; and, confounding farther these two denominations, they have bestowed the name of *Moros* upon the Arabs of Morocco and those in the environs of Senegal.

The Arabs who invaded Northern Africa about 650, were all natives of Asia, belonging to various provinces of Arabia, and were divided into Ismaelites, Amalekites, Koushites, &c. They were all warriors; and it is considered a title of nobility to have belonged to their first irruption of the enthusiastic sons of the Prophet.

A second invasion took place towards the end of the ninth century—an epoch full of wars—during which, the Caliph Kaïm transported the seat of his government from Kairwan to Cairo,

---

Others, and with more probability, derive it from *Sharak*, the east, and make them Orientals, and others say there is an Arabic word *Saracini*, which means a pastoral people, and assert that Saracine is a corruption from it, the new Arabian immigrants being supposed to have been pastoral tribes.

ending in the complete submission of Morocco to the power of Yousef Ben Tashfin. One cannnot now distinguish which tribe of Arabs belong to the first or the second invasion, but all who can shew the slightest proof, claim to belong to the first, as ranking among a band of noble and triumphant warriors.

After eight centuries of rule, the Arabs being expelled from Spain, took refuge in Barbary, but instead of finding the hospitality and protection of their brethren, the greater part of them were pillaged or massacred. The remnant of these wretched fugitives settled along the coast; and it is to their industry and intelligence that we owe the increase, or the foundation of many of the maritime cities. Here, considered as strangers and enemies by the natives, whom they detested, the new colonists sought for, and formed relations with Turks and renegades of all nations, whilst they kept themselves separate from the Arabs and Berbers. This, then, is the *bonâ-fide* origin of the people whom we now generally call Moors. History furnishes us with a striking example of how the expelled Arabs of Spain united with various adventurers against the Berber and North African Arabs. In the year 1500, a thousand Andalusian cavaliers, who had emigrated to Algiers, formed an alliance with the Barbarossas and their fleet of pirates; and, after expelling the native prince, built the modern city of Algiers. And such was the origin of the Algerine Corsairs.

The general result of these observations would, therefore, lead us to consider the Moors of the Romans, as the Berbers or aborigines of North Africa, and the Moors of the Spaniards, as pure Arabians; and if, indeed, these Arabian cavaliers marshalled with them Berbers, as auxiliaries, for the conquest of Spain, this fact does not militate against the broad assumption.

The so-called Moors of Senegal and the Sahara, as well as those of Morocco, are chiefly a mixture of Berbers, Arabs and Negroes; but the present Moors located in the northern coast of Africa, are rather the descendants from the various conquering nations, and especially from renegades and Christian slaves.

The term Moors is not known to the natives themselves. The people speak definitely enough of Arabs and of various Berber tribes. The population of the towns and cities are called generally after the names of these towns and cities, whilst Tuniseen and Tripoline is applied to all the inhabitants of the great towns of Tunis and Tripoli. Europeans resident in Barbary, as a general rule, call all the inhabitants of towns—Moors, and the peasants or people residents in tents—Arabs. But, in Tripoli, I found whole villages inhabited by Arabs, and these I thought might be distinguished as town Arabs. Then the mountains of Tripoli are covered with Arab villages, and some few considerable towns are inhabited by people who are *bonâ-fide* Arabs. Finally, the capitals of North

Africa are filled with every class of people found in the country.

The question is then where shall we draw the line of distinction in the case of nationalities? or can we, with any degree of precision, define the limits which distinguish the various races in North Africa? With regard to the Blacks or negro tribes, there can be no great difficulty. The Jews are also easily distinguished from the rest of the people as well by their national features as by their dress and habits or customs of living. But, when we come to the Berbers, Arabs, Moors and Turks, we can only distinguish them in their usual and ordinary occupations and manners of life. Whenever they are intermixed, or whenever they change their position, that is to say, whenever the Arab or Berber comes to dwell in a town, or a Moor or a Turk goes to reside in the cou ry, adopting the Arab or Berber dress and mode of living, it is no longer possible to distinguish the one from the other, or mark the limitation of races.

And since it is seen that the aborigines of Northern Africa consisted, with the exception of the Negro tribes, of the Asiatics of the Caucasian race or variety, many of whom, like the Phœnicians, have peopled various cities and provinces of Europe, it is therefore not astonishing we should find all the large towns and cities of North Africa, where the human being becomes *policed*, refined and civilized sooner than in remote and thinly-inhabited districts, teeming with a population, which at once challenges an European type, and a corresponding origin with the great European family of nations.

North Africa is wonderfully homogeneous in the matter of religion. The people, indeed, have but one religion. Even the extraneous Judaism is the same in its Deism—depression of the female—circumcision and many of the religious customs, festivals and traditions. And this has a surprising effect in assimilating the opposite character and sharpest peculiarities of various races of otherwise distinct and independant origin.

The population of Morocco presents five distant races and classes of people: Berbers, Arabs, Moors, Jews and Negroes. Turks are not found in Morocco, and do not come so far west; but sons of Turks by Moorish women in Kouroglies are included among the Moors, that have emigrated from Algeria. Maroquine Berbers, include the varieties of the Amayeegh and the Shelouh, who mostly are located in the

* Some suppose that *Amayeegh* means "great," and the tribes thus distinguished themselves, as our neighbours are wont to do by the phrase "la grande nation." The Shoulah are vulgarly considered to be descended from the Philistines, and to have fled before Joshua on the conquest of Palestine.

In his translation of the Description of Spain, by the Shereef El-Edris (Madrid, 1799), Don Josef Antonio Conde speaks of the Berbers in a note—

"Masmuda, one of the five principal tribes of Barbaria; the others are Zeneta, called Zenetes in our novels and histories, Sanhagha which we name Zenagas; Gomêsa is spelt in our histories Gomares and Gomêles. Huroara, some of these were originally from Arabia; there were others, but not so

## 88  TRAVELS IN MOROCCO.

mountains, while the Arabs are settled on the plains.

The Moors are the inhabitants of towns and cities, consisting of a mixture of nearly all races, a great proportion of them being of the descendants of the Moors expelled from Spain. All these races have been, and will still be, farther noticed in the progress of the work.

distinguished. La de Ketâma was, according to tradition, African, one of the most ancient, for having come with Afrikio.

"Ben Kis Ben Taifi Ben Tebâ, the younger, who came from the king of the Assyrians, to the land of the west.

"None of these primitive tribes appear to have been known to the Romans, their historians, however, have transmitted to us many names of other aboriginal tribes, some of which resemble fractions now existing, as the Getules are probably the present Geudala or Geuzoula. But the present Berbers do not correspond with the names of the five original people just mentioned. In Morocco, there are Amaycegh and Shelouh, in Algeria the Kabyles, in Tunis the Aoures, sometimes the Shouwiah, and in Sahara the Touarichs. There are, besides, numerous subdivisions and admixtures of these tribes."

The proximate amount of this population is six millions. The greater number of the towns and cities are situate on the coast, excepting the three or four capitals, or imperial cities. The other towns of the interior should be considered rather as forts to awe neighbouring tribes, or as market villages (*souks*), where the people collect together for the disposal and exchange of their produce. Numerous tribes, located in the Atlas, escape the notice of the imposts of imperial authority. Their varieties and amount of population are equally unknown. In the immense group of Gibel Thelge (snowy mountains), some of the tribes are said to have their faces shaved, like Christians, and to wear boots. We can understand why a people inhabiting a cold region of rain and mists and perpetual snow should wear boots; but as to their shaving like Christians, this is rather vague. But it is not impossible the Atlas contains the descendants of some European refugees.

The nature of the soil and climate of Morocco

are not unlike those of Spain and Portugal; and though Morocco does not materially differ from other parts of Barbary, its greater extent of coast on the Atlantic, along which the trade-wind of the north coast blows nine months out of twelve, and its loftier ridges of the Atlas, so temper its varied surface of hill and plain and vast declivities that, together with the absence of those marshy districts which in hot climates engender fatal disease, this country may be pronounced, excepting perhaps Tunis, the most healthy in all Africa.

In the northern provinces, the climate is nearly the same as that of Spain; in the southern there is less rain and more of the desert heat, but this is compensated for by the greater fertility in the production of valuable staple articles of commerce. Nevertheless, Morocco has its extremes of heat and cold, like all the North African coast.

The most striking object of this portion of the crust of the globe, is the vast Atlas chain of mountains,* which traverses Morocco from north-east to south-west, whose present ascer-

* Monsieur Balbi is decidedly the most recent, as well as the best authority to apply to for a short and definite description of this most celebrated mountain system, called by him "Système Atlantique," and I shall therefore annex what he says on this interesting subject, "Orographie." He says—" Of the 'Système Atlantique,' which derives its name from the Mount Atlas, renowned for so many centuries, and still so little known; we include in this vast system, all the heights of the region of Maghreb—we mean the mountains of the Barbary States—as well as the elevations scattered in the immense Sahara or Desert. It appears that the most important ridge extends from the neighbourhood of Cape Noun, or the Atlantic, as far as the east of the Great Syrte in the State of Tripoli. In this vast space it crosses the new State of Sidi-Hesdham, the Empire of Morocco, the former State of Algiers, as well as the State of Tripoli and the Regency of Tunis. It is in the Empire of Morocco, and especially in the east of the town of Morocco, and in the south-east of Fez, that that ridge presents the greatest heights of the whole system. It goes on diminishing afterwards in height as it extends towards the east, so that it appears the summits of the territory of Algiers are higher than those on the territory of Tunis, and the latter are less high than those to be found in the State of Tripoli. Several secondary ridges

tained culminating point, Miltsin, is upwards of 15,000 feet above the level of the sea, or equal

diverge in different directions from the principal chain; we shall name among them the one which ends at the Strait of Gibraltar in the Empire of Morocco. Several intermediary mountains seem to connect with one another the secondary chains which intersect the territories of Algiers and Tunis. Geographers call Little Atlas the secondary mountains of the land of Sous, in opposition to the name of Great Atlas, they give to the high mountains of the Empire of Morocco. In that part of the principal chain called Mount Gharian, in the south of Tripoli, several low branches branch off and under the names of Mounts Maray, Black Mount Haroudje, Mount Liberty, Mount Tiggerandoumma and others less known, furrow the great solitudes of the Desert of Lybia and Sahara Proper. From observations made on the spot by Mr. Bruguière in the former state of Algiers, the great chain which several geographers traced beyond the Little Atlas under the name of Great Atlas does not exist. The inhabitants of Mediah who were questioned on the subject by this traveller, told him positively, that the way from that town to the Sahara was through a ground more or less elevated, and slopes more or less steep, and without having any chain of mountains to cross. The Pass of Teniah which leads from Algiers to Mediah is, therefore, included in the principal chain of that part of the Regency.

to the highest peaks of the Pyrenees. The Maroquine portion of the Atlas contains its highest peaks, which stretch from the east of Tripoli to the Atlantic Ocean, at Santa Cruz; and we find no mountains of equal height, except in the tenth degree of North latitude, or 18,000 miles south, or 30,000 south, south-east. The Rif coast has a mountainous chain of some considerable height, but the Atlantic coast offers chiefly ridges of hills. The coasts of Morocco are not much indented, and consequently have few ports, and these offer poor protection from the ocean.

The general surface of Morocco presents a large ridge or lock, with two immense declivities, one sloping N.W. to the ocean, with various rivers and streams descending from this enormous back-bone of the Atlas, and the other fulling towards the Sahara, S.E., feeding the streams and affluents of Wad Draha, and other rivers, which are lost in the sands of the Desert. This shape of the country prevents the formation of those vast *Sebhahas,* or salt lakes, so frequent in Algeria and the south of Tunis. We are acquainted only with two lakes of fresh or sweet water—that of Debaia, traversed by Wad Draha, and that of Gibel-Akhder, which Leo compares to Lake Bolsena. The height of the mountains, and the uniformity of their slopes, produce large and numerous rivers; indeed, the most considerable of all North Africa. These rivers of the North are shortest, but have the largest volume of water; those of the South are larger, but are nearly dry the greater part of the year. None of them are navigable far inland. Some abound with fish, particularly the Shebbel, or Barbary salmon. It is neither so rich nor so large as our salmon, and is white-fleshed; it tastes something like herring, but is of a finer and more delicate flavour. They are abundant in the market of Mogador. The Shebbel, converted by the Spaniards Sabalo, is found in the Guadalquivir.

The products of the soil are nearly the same

as in other parts of Barbary. On the plains, or in the open country, the great cultivation is wheat and barley; in suburban districts, vegetables and fruits are propagated. In a commercial point of view, the North exports cattle, grain, bark, leeches, and skins; and the South exports gums, almonds, ostrich-feathers, wax, wool, and skins, as principle staple produce. When the rains cease or fail, the cultivation is kept up by irrigation, and an excellent variety of fruits and esculent vegetables are produced; indeed, nearly all the vegetables and fruit-trees of Southern Europe are here abundantly and successfully cultivated, besides those peculiar to an African clime and soil. In the south, grows a tree peculiar to this country, the Elœondenron Argan, so called from its Arabic name Argan. This tree produces fruit resembling the olive, whose egg-shaped, brown, smooth and very hard stone, encloses a flat almond, of a white colour, and of a very disagreeable taste, which, when crushed, produces a rancid oil, used commonly as a substitute for olive-oil. The tree itself is bushy and large, and sometimes grows of the size to a wide-spreading oak. Not far from Mogador are several Argan forests. The level country of the north is covered with forests of dwarfish oak; some bear sweet, and others bitter acorns, and also the cork-tree, whose bark is a considerable object of commerce. In the Atlas, has been found the magnificent cedar of Lebanon. This tree has also been met with in Algeria, but only on the mountains, some forty thousand feet above the level of the sea.

In the South there is, of course, growing in all its Saharan vigour, the noble date-palm, and by its side, squats the palmetto, or dwarf-palm (in Arabic *dauma*). Of trees and plants, the usual tinzah, and snouber or pine of Aleppo, are used for preparing the fine leathers of Morocco. Many plants are also deleteriously employed for exciting intoxication, or inflaming the passions.

Morocco has its mines of gold, silver, lead, iron, tin, sulphur, mineral, salt, and antimony; but nearly all are neglected, or unworked Government will not encourage the industry of the people, for fear of exciting the cupidity of foreigners. A Frenchman, a short time ago, reported a silver mine in the south, and Government immediately bribed him to make another statement that there was no such mine. At Elala and Stouka, in the province of Sous, are several rich silver mines. Gold is found in the Atlas and the Lower Sous. But this country is especially rich in copper mines. A great number of ancient and modern authors speak of these mines, which are situate in the mountainous country comprised between Aghadir, Morocco, Talda, Tamkrout, and Akka. The mines most worked, are those of Tedsi and Afran. At the foot of the Atlas, near Taroudant, is a great quantity of sulphur. In the neighbourhood of Morocco, saltpetre is found. In the province of Abda is an extensive salt lake, and salt has been

VOL. II. H

exported from this country to Timbuctoo. Of precious stones, some fine specimens of amethyst have been discovered.

There are scarcely any animals peculiar to Morocco, or which are not found in other parts of North Africa. Davidson mentions some curious facts relative to the desert horse; *sherberrech*, wind-bibber, or drinker of the wind," a variety of this animal, which is not to be met with in the Saharan regions of Tunis, or Tripoli.

This horse is fed only on camel's milk, and is principally used for hunting ostriches, which are run down by it, and then captured.* The *sherb-errech* will continue running three or four days together without any food. It is a slight and spare-formed animal, mostly in wretched condition, with ugly thick legs, and devoid of beauty as a horse.

* Xenophon, in his Anabasis, speaks of ostriches in Mesopotamia being run down by fleet horses.

## CHAPTER IV.

Division of Morocco into kingdoms or States, and zones or regions.—Description of the towns and cities on the Maroquine coasts of the Mediterranean and Atlantic waters.—The Zafarine Isles.—Melilla.—Alhucemas.—Penon de Velez.—Tegaza.--Provinces of Rif and Garet.—Tetouan. —Ceuta. — Arzila. — El Araish. — Mehedia. — Salee.— Rabat. — Fidallah. — Dar-el-Beidah. — Azamour. — Mazagran.—Saffee.—Waladia.

Morocco has been divided into States, or kingdoms by Europeans, although such divisions scarcely exist in the administration of the native princes. The ancient division mentioned by Leo was that of two large provinces of Morocco and Fez, separated by the river Bouragrag, which empties itself into the sea between Rabat and Salee; and, indeed, for several centuries, these districts were separated and governed by independent princes. Tafilett always, and Sous occasionally, were united to Morocco, while Fez itself formed a powerful kingdom, extending itself eastward as far as the gates of Tlemsen.

The modern division adopted by several authors, is—

Northern, or the kingdom of Fez. Central, or the kingdom of Morocco. Eastern, or the Province of Tafilett. Southern, or the province of Sous. Some add to this latter, the Province of Draha.

Then, a great number of districts are enumerated as comprehended in these large and general divisions; but the true division of all Mussulman States is into tribes. There is besides another, which more approaches to European government, viz, into kaidats, or jurisdictions. The name of a district is usually that of its chief tribe, and mountains are denominated after the tribes that inhabit them. There is, of course, a natural division, sometimes called a dividing into zones or specific regions, which has already been alluded to in enumerating the natural resources of Morocco, and which besides corresponds with the present political divisions.

I. The North of the Atlas: coming first, the Rif, or mountainous region, which borders the Mediterranean from the river Moulwia to Tangier, comprising the districts of Hashbat west, and Gharet and Aklaia east. Then the intermediate zone of plains and hills, which extends from the middle course of the Moulwia to Tangier on one coast, and to Mogador on the other.

II. The Central Region, or the great chain of the Atlas. The Deren* of the natives, from

* Mount Atlas was called Dyris by the ancient aborigines, or Derem, its name amongst the modern aborigines. This word has been compared to the Hebrew, signifying the place

the frontiers of Algeria east to Cape Gheer, on the south-west. This includes the various districts of the Gharb, Temsna, Beni Hasan, Shawia, Fez, Todla, Dukala, Shragno, Abda, Haha, Shedma, Khamna, Morocco, &c.

III. South of the Atlas: or quasi-Saharan region, comprising the various provinces and districts of Sous, Sidi Hisham, Wadnoun, Guezoula, Draha (Drâa), Tafilett, and a large

or aspect of the sun at noon-day, as if Mount Atlas was the back of the world, or the cultivated parts of the globe, and over which the sun was seen at full noon, in all his fierce and glorious splendour. Bochart connects the term with the Hebrew meaning 'great' or 'mighty,' which epithet would be naturally applied to the Atlas, and all mountains, by either a savage or civilized people. We have, also, on the northern coast, Russadirum, the name given by the Moors to Cape Bon, which is evidently a compound of *Ras*, head, and *dirum*, mountain, or the head of the mountain.

We have again the root of this word in Doa-el-Hamman, Tibet Deera, &c., the names of separate chains of the mighty Atlas. Any way, the modern Der-en is seen to be the same with the ancient Dir-is.

portion of the Sahara, south-east of the Atlas.

As to statistics of population I am inclined fully to admit the statement of Signor Balbi that, the term of African statistics ought to be rejected as absurd. Count Hemo de Gräberg, who was a long time Consul at Tangier, and wrote a statistical and geographical account of the empire of Morocco, states the number of the inhabitants of the town of Mazagran to be two thousand. Mr. Elton who resided there several months, assured me it does not contain more than one hundred. Another gentleman who dwelt there says, three hundred. This case is a fair sample of the style in which the statistics of population in Morocco are and have been calculated.

Before the occupation of Algeria by the French, all the cities were vulgarly calculated at double, or treble their amount of population. This has also been the case even in India, where we could obtain, with care, tolerably correct statistics. The prejudices of oriental and Africo-eastern people are wholly set against statistics, or numbering the population. No mother knows the age of her own child. It is ill-omened, if not an affront, to ask a man how many children he has; and to demand the amount of the population of a city, is either constructed as an infringement upon the prerogative of the omnipotent Creator, who knows how many people he creates, and how to take care of them, or it is the question of a spy, who is seeking to ascertain the strength or weakness of the country. Europeans can, therefore, rarely obtain any correct statistical information in Morocco: all is proximate and conjectural.* I am anxious, nevertheless, to give some particulars respecting the population, in order that we may really have a proximate idea of the strength and

* The only way of obtaining any information at all, is through the registers of taxation; and, to the despotism and exactions of these and most governments, we owe a knowledge of the proximate amount of the numbers of mankind.

resources of this important country. In describing the towns and cities of the various provinces, I shall divide them into,

1. Towns and cities of the coast.
2. Capital or royal cities.
3. Other towns and remarkable places in the interior.*

The towns and ports, on the Mediterranean, are of considerable interest, but our information is very scanty, except as far as relates to the *praesidios* of Spain, or the well-known and much frequented towns of Tetuan and Tangier.

Near the mouth of the Malwia (or fifteen miles distant), is the little town of Kalat-el-wad, with a castle in which the Governor resides. Whether the river is navigable up to this place, I have not been able to discover. The water-communication of the interior of North Africa is not worth the name.

---

\* Tangier, Mogador, Wadnoun, and Sous have already been described, wholly, or in part.

Zaffarinds or Jafarines, are three isles lying off the west of the river Mulweeah, at a short distance, or near its mouth. These belong to Spain, and have recently been additionally fortified, but why, or for what reason, is not so obvious. Opposite to them, there is said to be a small town, situate on the mainland. The Spaniards, in the utter feebleness and decadence of their power, have lately dubbed some one or other " Captain-general of the Spanish possessions, &c. in North Africa."

Melilla or Melilah is a very ancient city, founded by the Carthaginians, built near a cape called by the Romans, *Rusadir* (now Tres-Forcas) the name afterwards given to the city, and which it still retains in the form of Ras-ed-Dir, (Head of the mountain). This town is the capital of the province of Garet, and is said to contain 3,000 souls. It is situate amidst a vast tract of fine country, abounding in minerals, and most delicious honey, from which it is pretended the place receives its name.

On an isle near, and joined to the mainland by a draw-bridge, is the Spanish *praesidio,* or convict-settlement called also Melilla, containing a population of 2,244 according to the Spanish, but Rabbi and Gräberg do not give it more than a thousand. At a short distance, towards the east, is an exceedingly spacious bay, of twenty-two miles in circumference, where, they say, a thousand ships of war could be anchored in perfect safety, and where the ancient galleys of Venice carried on a lucrative trade with Fez. Within the bay, three miles inland, are the ruins of the ancient city of Eazaza, once a celebrated place.

Alhucemos, is another small island and *praesidio* of the Spaniards, containing five or six hundred inhabitants; it commands the bay of the same name, and is situate at the mouth of the river Wad Nechor, where there is also the Islet of Ed-Housh. Near the bay, is the ancient capital, Mezemma, now in ruins; it had, however, some commercial importance in the times of Louis XIV., and carried on trade with France.

Peñon de Velez is the third *praesidio*-island, a convict settlement of the Spaniards on this coast, and a very strong position, situate opposite the mouths of the river Gomera, which disembogues in the Mediterranean. The garrison contains some nine hundred inhabitants. So far as natural resources are concerned, Peñon de Velez is a mere rock, and a part of the year is obliged to be supplied with fresh water from the mainland. Immediately opposite to the continent is the city of Gomera (or Badis), the ancient Parientina, or perhaps the Acra of Ptolemy, afterwards called Belis, and by the Spaniards, Velez de la Gomera. The name Gomera, according to J. A. Conde, is derived from the celebrated Arab tribe of the Gomeres, who flourished in Africa and Spain until the last Moorish kings of Granada. Count Gräberg pretends Gomera now contains three thousand inhabitants! whilst other writers, and of later date, represent this ancient city, which has flourished and played an important part through many ages, as entirely abandoned, and the abode of serpents and hyænas. Gellis is a small port, six miles east of Velez de Gomera.

Tegaza is a small town and port, at two miles or less from the sea near Pescadores Point, inhabited mostly by fishermen, and containing a thousand souls.

The provinces of Rif and Garet, containing these maritime towns are rich and highly cultivated, but inhabited by a warlike and semi-barbarous race of Berbers, over whom the Emperor exercises an extremely precarious authority. Among these tribes, Abd-el-Kader sought refuge and support when he was obliged to retire from Algeria, and, where he defied all the power of the Imperial government for several months. Had the Emir chosen, he could have remained in Rif till this time; but he determined to try his strength with the Sultan in a pitch battle, which should decide his fate.

The savage Rifians assemble for barter and trade on market-days, which are occasions of fierce and incessant quarrels among themselves, when it is not unusual for two or three persons to be left dead on the spot. Should any unfortunate vessel strike on these coasts, the crew find themselves in the hands of inhuman wreckers. No European traveller has ever visited these provinces, and we may state positively that journeying here is more dangerous than in the farthest wastes of the Sahara. Spanish renegades, however, are found among them, who have escaped from the *praesidios*, or penal settlements. The Rif country is full of mines, and is bounded south by one of the lesser chains of the Atlas running parallel with the coast. Forests of cork clothe the mountain-slopes; the Berbers graze their herds and flocks in the deep green valleys, and export quantities of skins.

Tetuan, the Yagath of the Romans, situate at the opening of the Straits of Gibraltar, four or five miles from the sea, upon the declivity of a hill and within two small ranges of mountains, is a fine, large, rich and mercantile city of the province of Hasbat. It has a resident governor of considerable power and consequence, the name of the present functionary being Hash-Hash, who has long held the appointment, and enjoys great influence near the Sultan. Half a mile east of the city passes from the south Wad Marteen, (the Cus of Marmol) which disembogues into the sea; on its banks is the little port of Marteen or Marteel, not quite two miles distant from the coast, and about three from the city, where a good deal of commerce is carried on, small vessels, laden with the produce of Barbary, sailing thence to Spain, Gibraltar, and even France and Italy. The population of Tetouan is from nine to twelve thousand souls, including, besides Moors and Arabs, four thousand Jews, two thousand

Negroes, and eight thousand Berbers. The streets are generally formed into arcades, or covered bazaars.

The Jews have a separate quarter; their women are celebrated for their beauty. The suburbs are adorned with fine gardens, and olive and vine plantations. Orange groves, or rather orange forests, extend for miles around, yielding their golden treasures. A great export of oranges could be established here, which might be conveyed overland to India. Altogether, Tetuan is one of the most respectable coast-cities of Morocco, though it has no port immediately adjoining it. Its fortifications are only strong enough to resist the attack of hostile Berbers. The town is about two-thirds of a day's journey from Tangier, south-east. A fair day's journey would be, in Morocco, upwards of thirty English miles, but a good deal depends upon the season of the year when you travel.

Ceuta is considered to be Esilissa of Ptolemy,

and was once the capital of Mauritania Tingitana. The Arabs call it Sebât and Sebta, *i.e.*, " seven," after the Romans, who called it *Septem fratres*, and the Greeks the same, apparently on account of the seven mountains, which are in the neighbourhood. Ceuta, or Sebta, is evidently the modern form of this classic name. It is a very ancient city and celebrated fortress, situate fourteen miles south of Gibraltar, nearly opposite to it, as a species of rival stronghold, and placed upon a peninsula, which detaches itself from the continent on the east, and turns then to the north. The city extends over the tongue of land nearest the continent; the citadel occupies Monte-del-Acho, called formerly Jibel-el-Mina, a name still preserved in Almina, a suburb to the south-east.

In the beginning of the eighth century, Ceuta, which was inhabited by the Goths, passed into the hands of the Arabs, who made it a point of departure for the expeditions into Spain. It was conquered by the powerful Arab family of the Ben-Hamed, one of whom, called Mohammed Edris, invaded Spain, and, after several conquests, was proclaimed King of Cordova, in A.D. 1,000.

On 21st of August, 1415, the Portuguese conquered it, and it was the first place which they occupied in Africa. In 1578, at the death of Don Sebastian, Ceuta passed with Portugal and the rest of the colonies into the power of Spain; and when, in 1640, the Portuguese recovered their independence, the Spaniards were left masters of Ceuta, which continues still in their hands, but is of no utility to them except as a *praesidio*, which makes the fourth penal settlement possessed by them on this coast.

Ceuta contains a garrison of two or three thousand men. The free population amounts to some five or six thousand. It has a small and insecure port. Here is the famed Gibel Zaterit, "Monkey's promontory," or " Ape's Hill," which has occasioned the ingenious fable, that, inasmuch as there are no monkeys in any part of Europe except Gibraltar, directly opposite to this rock, where also monkeys are found, there must necessarily be a subterranean passage beneath the sea, by which they pass and re-pass to opposite sides of the Straits, and maintain a friendly and uninterrupted intercourse between the brethren of Africa and Europe. Anciently, the mountains hereabouts formed the African pillars of Hercules opposite to Gibraltar, which may be considered the European pillar of that respectable hero of antiquity.

Passing Tangier after a day's journey, we come to Arzila or Asila, in the province of Hasbat, which is an ancient Berber city, and which, when conquered by the Romans, was named first Zilia and afterwards Zulia, Constantia Zilis. It is placed on the naked shores of the Atlantic, and has a little port. Whilst possessed by the Portuguese, it was a place of considerable strength, but its fortifications being, as usual, neglected by the Moors, are now rapidly decaying.* The population is about one thousand. The country around produces good tobacco. The next town on the Atlantic, after another day's journey southwards, is El Araish, *i.e.*, the trellices of vines; vulgarly called Laratsh. This city replaces the ancient Liscas or Lixus and Lixa, whose ruins are near. The Arabs call it El-Araish Beni-Arous, *i.e.*, the vineyards of the Beni-Arous, a powerful tribe, who populate the greater part of the district of Azgar, of which it is the capital and the residence of the Governor. It was, probably, built by this tribe about 1,200 or 1,300, A.D. El-Araish contains a population of 2,7000 Moors, and 1,300 Jews, or 4,000 souls; but others give only 2,000 for the whole amount, of which 250 are Jews. It has a garrison of 500 troops. The town is situate upon a small promontory stretching into the sea, and along the mouth of the river Cos, or

* In 936, Arzila was sacked by the English, and remained for twenty years uninhabited.

Luccos (Loukkos), which forms a secure port, but of so difficult access, that vessels of two hundred tons can scarcely enter it. In winter, the roadstead is very bad;* the houses are substantially built; and the fortifications are good, because made by the Spaniards, who captured this place in 1610, but it was re-taken by Muley Ishmael in 1689. The climate is soft

---

* According to Mr. Hay, a portion of the Salee Rovers seem to have finally taken refuge here. Up the river El-Kous, the Imperial squadron lay in ordinary, consisting of a corvette, two brigs, (once merchant-vessels, and which had been bought of Christians), and a schooner, with some few gun-boats, and even these two or three vessels were said to be all unfit for sea. But, when Great Britain captured the rock of Gibraltar, we, supplanting the Moors became the formidable toll-keepers of the Herculean Straits, and the Salee rivers have ever since been in our power. If the Shereefs have levied war or tribute on European navies since that period, it has been under our tacit sanction. The opinion of Nelson is not the less true, that, should England engage in war with any maritime State of Europe, Morocco must be our warm and active friend or enemy, and, if our enemy, we must again possess ourselves of our old garrison of Tangier.

and delicious. In the environs, cotton is cultivated, and charcoal is made from the Araish forest of cork-trees. El-Araish exports cork, wool, skins, bark, beans, and grain, and receives in exchange iron, cloth, cottons, muslins, sugar and tea. The lions and panthers of the mountains of Beni Arasis sometimes descend to the plains to drink, or carry off a supper of a sheep or bullock. Azgar, the name of this district, connects it with one of the powerful tribes of the Touaricks; and, probably, a section of this tribe of Berbers were resident here at a very early period (at the same time the Berber term *ayghar* corresponds to the Arabic *bahira*, and signifies " plain.")

The ancient Lixus deserves farther mention on account of the interest attached to its coins, a few of which remain, although but very recently deciphered by archeologists. There are five classes of them, and all Phœnician, although the city now under Roman rule, represents the vineyard riches of this part of ancient Mauritania by two bunches of grapes, so that, after nearly three thousand years, the place has retained its peculiarity of producing abundant vines, El-Araish, being "the vine trellices;" others have stamped on them "two ears of corn" and "two fishes," representing the fields of corn waving on the plains of Morocco, and the fish (shebbel especially) which fills its northern rivers.

Strabo says:—" Mauritania generally, excepting a small part desert, is rich and fertile, well watered with rivers and washed with lakes; abounding in all things, and producing trees of great dimensions." Another writer adds " this country produces a species of the vine whose trunk the extended arms of two men cannot embrace, and which yields grapes of a cubit's length." " At this city," says Pliny, " was the palace of Antæus, and his combat with Hercules and the gardens of Hesperides."

Mehedia or Mâmora, and sometimes, Nuova Mamora, is situate upon the north-western slope of a great hill, some four feet above the sea, upon the left bank of the mouth of the Sebon, and at the edge of the celebrated plain and forest of Mamora, belonging to the province of Beni-Hassan. According to Marmol, Mamora was built by Jakob-el-Mansour to defend the embouchure of the river. It was captured by the Spaniards in 1614, and retaken by the Moors in 1681. The Corsairs formerly took refuge here. It is now a weak and miserable place, commanded by an old crumbling-down castle. There are five or six hundred fishermen, occupying one hundred and fifty cabins, who make a good trade of the Shebbel salmon; it has a very small garrison. The forest of Mamora, contains about sixty acres of fine trees, among which are some splendid oaks, all suitable for naval construction.

Salee or Sala, a name which this place bore antecedently to the Roman occupation, is a very ancient city, situate upon the right bank of the river Bouragrag, and near its mouth. This place was captured in 1263, by Alphonso the Wise, King of Castille, who was a short time after dispossessed of his conquest by the King of Fez; and the Moorish Sultans have kept it to the present time, though the city itself has often attempted to throw off the imperial yoke. The modern Salee is a large commercial and well-fortified city of the province of Beni-Hassan. Its port is sufficiently large, but, on account of the little depth of water, vessels of large burden cannot enter it. The houses and public places are tolerably well-built. The town is fortified by a battery of twenty-four pieces of cannon fronting the sea, and a redoubt at the entrance of the river. What navy the Maroquines have, is still laid up here, but the dock-yard is now nearly deserted, and the few remaining ships are unserviceable. The population, all of whom are Mahometans, are now, as in Corsair times, the bitterest and most determined enemies of Christians, and will not permit a Christian or Jew to reside among them. The amount of this population, and that of Rabat, is thus given,

|  | Salee | Rabat |
|---|---|---|
| Gräberg | 23,000 | 27,000 |
| Washington | 9,000 | 21,000 |
| Arlett | 14,000 | 24,000 |

but it is probably greatly exaggerated.

A resident of this country reduces the population of Salee as low as two or three thousand. For many years, the port of Salee was the rendezvous of the notorious pirates of Morocco, who, together with the city of Rabat, formed a species of military republic almost independent of the Sultan; these Salee rovers were at once the most ferocious and courageous in the world. Time was, when these audacious freebooters lay under Lundy Island in the British Channel, waiting to intercept British traders! "Salee," says Lemprière, "was a place of good commerce, till, addicting itself entirely to piracy, and revolting from the allegiance to its Sovereign, Muley Zidan, that prince in the year 1648, dispatched an embassy to King Charles I, of England, requesting him to send a squadron of men-of-war to lie before the town, while he attacked by land." This request being acceded to, the city was soon reduced, the fortifications demolished, and the leaders of the rebellion put to death. The year following, the Emperor sent another ambassador to England, with a present of Barbary horses and three hundred Christian slaves.

Rabat, or Er-Rabat, and on some of the foreign maps Nuova Sale, is a modern city of considerable extent, densely populated, strong and well-built, belonging to the province of Temsna. It is situate on the declivity of a hill, opposite to Salee, on the other side of the river, or left side of the Bouragrag, which is as broad as the Thames at London Bridge, and might be considered as a great suburb, or another quarter of the same city. It was built by the famous

Yakob-el-Mansour, nephew of Abd-el-Moumen, and named by him Rabat-el-Fatah, *i. e.*, "camp of victory," by which name it is now often mentioned.

The walls of Rabat enclose a large space of ground, and the town is defended on the seaside by three forts, erected some years ago by an English renegade, and furnished with ordnance from Gibraltar. Among the population are three or four thousand Jews, some of them of great wealth and consequence. The merchants are active and intelligent, carrying on commerce with Fez, and other places of the interior, as also with the foreign ports of Genoa, Gibraltar, and Marseilles. In the middle ages, the Genoese had a great trade with Rabat, but this trade is now removed to Mogador. Many beautiful gardens and plantations adorn the suburbs, deserving even the name of "an earthly paradise."

The Moors of Rabat are mostly from Spain, expelled thence by the Spaniards. The famous

Sultan, Almanzor, intended that Rabat should be his capital. His untenanted mausoleum is placed here, in a separate and sacred quarter. This prince, surnamed " the victorious," (Elmansor,) was he who expelled the Moravedi from Spain. He is the Nero of Western Africa, as Keatinge says, their " King Arthur." Tradition has it that Elmansor went in disguise to Mecca, and returned no more. Mankind love this indefinite and obscure end of their heroes. Moses went up to the mountain to die there in eternal mystery. At a short distance from Rabat is Shella, or its ruins, a small suburb situate on the summit of a hill, which contains the tombs of the royal family of the Beni-Merini, and the founder of Rabat, and is a place of inviolate sanctity, no infidel being permitted to enter therein. Monsieur Chénier supposes Shella to have been the site of the metropolis of the Carthaginian colonies.

Of these two cities, on the banks of the Wad-Bouragrag, Salee was, according to D'Anville, always a place of note as at the present time, and the farthest Roman city on the coast of the Atlantic, being the frontier town of the ancient Mauritania Tingitana. Some pretend that all the civilization which has extended itself beyond this point is either Moorish, or derived from European colonists. The river Wad-Bouragrag is somewhat a natural line of demarcation, and the products and animals of the one side differ materially from those of the other, owing to the number and less rapid descent of the streams on the side of the north, and so producing more humidity, whilst the south side, on the contrary, is of a higher and drier soil.

Fidallah, or Seid Allah, *i. e.*, " grace," or " gift of God," is a maritime village of the province of Temsa, founded by the Sultan Mohammed in 1773. It is a strong place, and surrounded with walls. Fidallah is situate on a vast plain, near the river Wad Millah, where there is a small port, or roadstead, to which the corsairs were wont to resort when they could not reach Salee, long before the village was built, called Mersa Fidallah. The place contains a thousand souls, mostly in a wretched condition. Sidi Mohammed, before he built Mogador, had the idea of building a city here; the situation is indeed delightful, surrounded with fertility.

Dar-el-Beida (or Casa-Blanco, " white house,") is a small town, formerly in possession of the Portuguese, who built it upon the ruins of Anfa or Anafa,* which they destroyed in 1468. They, however, scarcely finished it when they abandoned it in 1515. Dar-el-Beida is situate on the borders of the fertile plains of the province of Shawiya, and has a small port, formed by a river and a spacious bay on the Atlantic. The Romans are said to have built the ancient Anafa, in whose time it was a considerable place, but now it scarcely contains above a thousand inhabitants, and some reduce them to

* So called, it is supposed, from the quantity of aniseed grown in the neighbourhood.

two hundred. Sidi Mohammed attempted this place, and the present Sultan endeavoured to follow up these efforts. A little commerce with Europe is carried on here. The bay will admit of vessels of large burden anchoring in safety, except when the wind blows strong from the north-west. Casa Blanco is two days journey from Rabat, and twe from

Azamor, or Azemmour, which is an ancient and fine city of the province of Dukaila, built by the Amazigh Berbers, in whose language it signifies "olives." It is situate upon a hill, about one hundred feet above the sea, and distant half a mile from the shore, not far from the mouth of the Wad-Omm-er-Rbia (or Omm-Erbegh) on its southern bank, and is everywhere surrounded by a most fertile soil. Azamor contains now about eight or nine hundred inhabitants, but formerly was much more populated. The Shebbel salmon is the principal commerce, and a source of immense profit to the town. The river is very deep and rapid, so that the passage with boats is both difficult and dangerous. It is frequently of a red colour, and charged with slime like the Nile at the period of its inundations. The tide is felt five or six leagues up the river, according to Chénier. Formerly, vessels of every size entered the river, but now its mouth has a most difficult bar of sand, preventing large vessels going up, like nearly all the Maroquine ports situate on the mouths, or within the rivers.

Azamor was taken by the Portuguese under the command of the Duke of Braganza in 1513 who strengthened it by fortifications, the walls of which are still standing; but it was abandoned a century afterwards, the Indies having opened a more lucrative field of enterprise than these barren though honourable conquests on the Maroquine coast. This place is half a day's journey, or about fourteen miles from

Mazagran, *i. e.* the above Amayeeghs, an extremely ancient and strong castle, erected on a peninsula at the bottom of a spacious and excellent bay. It was rebuilt by the Portuguese in 1506, who gave it the name of Castillo Real. The site has been a centre of population from the remotest period, chiefly Berbers, whose name it still bears. The Arabs, however, call it El-Bureeja, *i. e.*, "the citadel." The Portuguese abandoned it in 1769; Mazagran was the last stronghold which they possessed in Morocco. The town is well constructed, and has a wall twelve feet thick, strengthened with bastions, There is a small port, or dock, on the north side of the town, capable of admitting small vessels, and the roadstead is good, where large vessels can anchor about two miles off the shore. Its traffic is principally with Rabat, but there is also some export trade to foreign parts. Its population is two or three hundred.* After

---

* Near Cape Blanco is the ruined town of Tit or Tet, supposed to be of Carthaginian origin, and once also possessed by the Portuguese, when commerce therein flourished.

proceeding two days south-west, you arrive at

Saffee, or properly Asafee, called by the natives Asfee, and anciently Soffia or Saffia, is a city of great antiquity, belonging to the province of Abda, and was built by the Carthaginians near Cape Pantin. Its site lies between two hills, in a valley which is exposed to frequent inundations. The roadsted of Saffee is good and safe during summer, and its shipping once enabled it to be the centre of European commerce on the Atlantic coast. The population amounts to about one thousand, including a number of miserable Jews. The walls of Saffee are massy and high. The Portuguese captured this city in 1508, voluntarily abandoning it in 1641. The country around is not much cultivated, and presents melancholy deserts; but there is still a quantity of corn grown. About forty miles distant, S.E., is a large salt lake. Saffee is one and a half day's journey from Mogador.

Equidistant between Mazagran and Saffee is

the small town of El-Waladia, situate on an extensive plain. Persons report that near this spot is a spacious harbour, or lagune, sufficiently capacious to contain four or five hundred sail of the line; but, unfortunately, the entrance is obstructed by some rocks, which, however, it is added, might easily be blown up. The lagune is also exposed to winds direct for the ocean. The town, enclosed within a square wall, and containing very few inhabitants, is supposed to have been built in the middle of the seventeenth century by the Sultan Waleed, after whom it was named.

This brings us to Mogador, which, with Aghadir, have already been described.

## CHAPTER V.

Description of the Imperial Cities or Capitals of the Empire. —El-Kesar.—Mequinez.—Fez.—Morocco.—The province of Tafilett, the birth-place of the present dynasty of the Shereefs.

The royal or capitals of the interior now demand our attention, which are El-Kesar, Mequinez, Fez, and Morocco.

El-Kesar, or Al-Kesar,* styled also El-Kesue-Kesar, is so named and distinguished because it owes its enlargement to the famous Sultan of

* El-Kesar is a very common name of a fortified town, and is usually written by the Spaniards Alcazar, being the name of the celebrated royal palace at Seville.

Fez, Almansor, who improved and beautified it about the year 1180, and designed this city as a magazine and rendezvous of troops for the great preparations he was making at the time for the conquest of Granada. El-Kesar is in the province of the Gharb, and situate on the southern bank of the Luccos; here is a deep and rapid stream, flowing W.$\frac{1}{4}$ N.W. The town is nearly as large as Tetuan, but the streets are dirty and narrow, and many of the houses in a ruinous condition. This fortified place was once adorned by some fifteen mosques, but only two or three are now fit for service. The population does not exceed four or five thousand souls, and some think this number over-estimated.

The surrounding country is flat meadow-land, but flooded after the rains, and producing fatal fevers, though dry and hot enough in summer. The suburban fields are covered with gardens and orchards. It was at El-Kesar, where, in A.D. 1578, the great battle of The Three Kings came off, because, besides the

Portuguese King, Don Sebastian, two Moorish princes perished on this fatal day. But one of them, Muley Moluc, died very ill in a litter, and was not killed in the fight; his death, however, was kept a secret till the close of the battle, in order that the Moors might not be discouraged. With their prince, Don Sebastian, perished the flower of the Portuguese nobility and chivalry of that time. War, indeed, was found " a dangerous game" on that woful day: both for princes and nobles, and many a poor soul was swept away

"Floating in a purple tide."

But the "trade of war" has been carried on ever since, and these lessons, written in blood, are as useless to mankind as those dashed off by the harmless pen of the sentimental moralist. El-Kesar is placed in Latitude, 35° 1 10" N.; Longitude, 5° 49' 30" W.

Mequinez,* in Arabic, Miknas (or Miknasa),

* Marmol makes this city to have succeeded the ancient

is a royal residence, and city of the province of Fez, situate upon a hill in the midst of a well-watered and most pleasant town, blessed with a pure and serene air. The city of Miknas is both large and finely built, of considerable interest and of great antiquity. It was founded by the tribe of Berbers Meknâsah, a fraction of the Zenatah, in the middle of the tenth century, and called Miknasat, hence is derived its present name. The modern town is surrounded with a triple wall thirteen feet high and three thick, enclosing a spacious area. This wall is mounted with batteries to awe the Berbers of the neighbouring mountains. The population amounts to about twenty thousand souls, (some say forty or fifty thousand) in which are included about nine thousand Negro troops, constituting the greater portion

---

Roman town of Silda or Gilda. Mequinez has been called Ez-Zetounah, from the immense quantities of olives in its immediate vicinity.

of the Imperial guard. Two thousand of these black troops are in charge of the royal treasures, estimated at some fifty millions of dollars, and always increasing. These treasures consist of jewels, bars of gold and silver, and money in the two precious metals, the greater part being Spanish and Mexican dollars.

The inhabitants are represented as being the most polished of the Moors, kind and hospitable to strangers. The palace of the Emperor is extremely simple and elegant, all the walls of which are *embroidered* with the beautiful stucco-work of Arabesque patterns, as pure and chaste as the finest lace. The marble for the pillars was furnished from the ruins adjacent, called Kesar Faraour, "Castle of Pharoah" (a name given to most of the old ruins of Morocco, of whose origin there is any doubt).

During the times of piracy, there was here, as also at Morocco, a Spanish hospitium for the ransom and recovery of Christian slaves. Even before Mequinez was constituted a royal city, it was a place of considerable trade and riches. Nothing of any peculiar value has been discovered among the extensive and ancient ruins abont a mile distant, and which have furnished materials for the building of several royal cities; they are, however, supposed to be Roman. Scarcely a day's journey separates Mequinez from Fez. It is not usual for two royal cities to be placed so near together, but which must render their fortunes inseparable.

Fez, or Fas. According to some, the name Fas, which signifies in Arabia a pickaxe, was given to it because one was found in digging its foundations. Others derive it from Fetha, silver. It is no longer the marvellous city described by Leo Africanus, yet its learning, wealth, and industry place it in the first rank of the cities of Morocco. During the eighth century, the Arabs, masters of Tunis, of all

Algeria, and the maritime cities of Morocco, seemed to think only of invading Europe and consolidating their power in Spain; but at this epoch, a descendant of Ali and Fatima, Edris Ben Abdalluh, quitted Arabia, passed into Morocco, and established himself at Oualili, the capital, where he remained till his death, and where he was buried. His character was generally known and venerated for its sanctity, and drew upon him the affectionate regard of the people, and all instinctively placed themselves near him as a leader of the Faithful, likely to put an end to anarchy, and establish order in the Mussulman world. His son, Edris-Ben-Edris, who inherited his virtues and influence, offering a species of ancient prototype to Abd-el Kader and his venerable father, Mahadin, was the first *bona-fide* Mussulman sovereign of the Maroquine empire, and founded Fez.

Fez is a most ancient centre of population, and had long been a famed city, before Muley

Edris, in the year A.D. 807 (others in 793), gave it its present form and character.

From that period, however, Fez* dates its modern celebrity and rank among the Mahometan capitals of the world, and especially as

* Don J. A. Conde says—"Fes or sea Fez, the capital of the realm of that name; the fables of its origin, and the grandeur of the Moors, who always speak of their cities as foundations of heroes, or lords of the whole world, &c., a foible of which our historians are guilty. Nasir-Eddin and the same Ullug Beig say, for certain, that Fez is the court of the king in the west. I must observe here, that nothing is less authentic than the opinions given by Casiri in his Library of the Escurial, that by the word Algarb, they always mean the west of Spain, and by the word Almagreb, the west of Africa; one of these appellations is generally used for the other. The same Casiri says, with regard to Fez, that it was founded by Edno Ben Abdallah, under the reign of Almansor Abu Giafar; he is quite satisfied with that assertion, but does not perceive that it contains a glaring anachronism. Fez was already a very ancient city before the Mohammed Anuabi of the Mussulmen, and Joseph, in his A. J., mentions a city of Mauritania; the prophet Nahum speaks of it also, when he addresses Ninive, he presents it as an example for No Ammon. He enumerates its districts and cities, and says, Fut and Lubim, Fez and Lybia, &c.

being the second city of Islamism, and the "palace of the Mussulmen Princes of the West." That the Spanish philologists should make Fut, of the Prophet Nahum, to be the ancient capital of Fez, is not remarkable, considering the numerous bands of emigrants, who, emerging from the coast, wandered as far as the pillars of Hercules; and, besides, in a country like North Africa, the theatre of so many revolutions, almost every noted city of the present period has had its ancient form, from which it has been successively changed.

The modern capital is placed in a valley upon the gentle slope of several hills by which it is surrounded, and whose heights are crowned with lovely gardens breathing odoriferous sweets. Close by is a little river, or a branch of the Tebou, named Wad-el-Juhor, or " streamlet," which supplies the city with excellent water.

The present buildings are divided into old and new Fez. The streets are so narrow that two men on horseback could scarcely ride abreast; they are, besides, very dark, and often arched over. Colonel Scott represents some of the streets, however, as a mile in length. The houses are high, but not handsome. The shops are numerous and much frequented, though not very fine in appearance. Fez contains no less than seven hundred mosques, fifty of which are superb, and ornamented with fine columns of marble; there is, besides, a hundred or more of very small and ill-built mosques, or rather, houses of prayer. The most famous of these temples of worship is El-Karoubin (or El-Karouïin), supported by three hundred pillars. In this is preserved the celebrated library of antiquity, where, it is pretended, ancient Greek and Latin authors are to be found in abundance with the lost books of Titus Livy.

This appears to be mere conjecture.* But the mosque the more frequented and venerated,

---

* I imagine we shall never know the truth of this until the French march an army into Fez, and sack the library.

is that dedicated to the founder of the city, Muley Edris, whose ashes repose within its sacred enclosure. So excessive is this "hero-worship" for this great sultan, that the people constantly invoke his name in their prayers instead of that of the Deity. The mausoleum of this sacro-santo prince is inviolable and unapproachable. The university of Fez was formally much celebrated, but little of its learning now remains. Its once high-minded orthodox mulahs are now succeeded by a fanatic and ignorant race of marabouts. Nevertheless, the few *hommes de lettres* found in Morocco are congregated here, and the literature of the empire is concentrated in this city. Seven large public schools are in full activity, besides numbers of private seminaries of instruction. The low humour of the talebs, and the fanaticism of the people, are unitedly preserved and developed in this notorious doggerel couplet, universally diffused throughout Morocco :—

*Ensara fee Senara*
*Elhoud fee Sefoud*
" Christians on the hook
Jews on the spit," or
" Let Christians be hooked,
And let Jews be cooked."

The great division of the Arabic into eastern and western dialects makes little real difference in a practical point of view. The Mogrebbin, or western, is well understood by all travellers, and, of course, by all scholars from the East.

The palace of the Sultan is not large, but is handsome. There are numerous baths, and an hospital for the mad or incurable. The population was estimated, not long ago, at 88,000 souls, of which there were 60,000 Moors and Arabs (the Moors being chiefly immigrants from Spain), 10,000 Berbers, 8,000 Jews, and 10,000 Negroes. But this amount has been reduced to 40,000, or even 30,000; and the probability is, the present population of Fez does not by any means, exceed 50,000, if it reaches that number. Nearly all the Jews reside in the new city, which, by its position, dominates the old one. The inhabitants of Fez, in spite of their learning and commerce, are distinguished for their fanaticism; and an European, without an escort of troops, cannot walk in the streets unless disguised. It was lately the head-quarters of the fanatics who preached " the holy war," and involved the Emperor in hostilities with the French.

The immense trade of every kind carried on at Fez gives it almost the air of an European city. In the great square, called Al-Kaisseriah, is exhibited all the commerce of Europe and Africa—nay, even of the whole world. The crowd of traffickers here assemble every day as at a fair. Fez has two annual caravans; one leaves for Central Africa, or Timbuctoo; and another for Mecca, or the caravan of pilgrims. The two great stations and rendezvous points of the African caravan are Tafilett and Touat. The journey from Fez to Timbuctoo occupies about ninety days. The Mecca caravan proceeds the same route as far as Touat, and then turns back north-east to Ghadames, Fezzan, and Angelah, and thence to Alexandria, which it accomplishes in four or five, to six months. All depends on the inclination of the Shereef, or Commandant, of the caravan; but the journey from Fez to Alexandria cannot, by the quickest caravan, be accomplished in much less time than three months and a half, or one hundred days. The value of the investments in this caravan has been estimated at a million of dollars; for the faithful followers of the Prophet believe, with us, that godliness is profitable in the life that now is, as well as in that which is to come.

Fez is surrounded with a vast wall, but which is in decay. What is this decay! It applies almost to every Moorish city and public building in North Africa. And yet the faith of the false prophet is as strong as ever, and with time and hoary age seems to strike its roots deeper into the hearts of its simple, but enthusiastic and duped devotees!

The city has seven gates, and two castles, at the east and west, form its main defence. These castles are very ancient, and are formed and supported by square walls about sixty feet in front, Ali Bey says, subterraneous passages are reported to exist between these castles and the city; and, whenever the people revolt against the Sultan, cannon are planted on the castles with a few soldiers as their guard. The fortifications, or Bastiles, of Paris, we see, therefore, were no new invention of Louis Philippe to awe the populace. The maxims of a subtle policy are instructive in despotism of every description.

The constituted authorities of Fez are like those of every city of Morocco. The Governor is the lieutenant of the sovereign, exercising the executive power; the Kady, or supreme judge, is charged with the administration oft he law, and the Al-Motassen fixes the price of provisions, and decides all the questions of trade and customs. There are but few troops at Fez, for it is not a strong military possession; on the contrary, it is commanded by accessible heights and is exposed to a *coup-de-main*.

Fez, indeed, could make no *bonâ-fide* resistance to an European army. The manufactures are principally woollen haiks, silk handkerchiefs, slippers and shoes of excellent leather, and red caps of felt, commonly called the fez; the first fabrication of these red caps appears to have been in this city. The Spanish Moorish immigrants introduced the mode of dressing goat and sheep-skins, at first known by the name of Cordovan from Cordova; but, since the Moorish forced immigration, they have acquired the celebrated name of Morocco. The chief food of the people is the national Moorish dish of *cuscasou*, a fine grained paste, cooked by steam, with melted fat, oil, or other liquids poured upon the dish, and sometimes garnished with pieces of fowl and other meat. A good deal of animal food is consumed, but few vegetables. The climate is mild in the winter, but suffocating with heat in the summer. This city is placed in latittude 34° 6′ 3″ N. longitude 4° 38″ 15′ W.

Morocco, or strictly in Arabic, *Maraksh*, which signifies " adorned," is the capital of the South, and frequently denominated the capital of the Empire, but it is only a *triste* shadow of its former greatness. It is sometimes honoured with the title of " the great city," or " country." Morocco occupies an immense area of ground, being seven miles in circumference, the interior of which is covered with heaps of ruins or more pleasantly converted into gardens. Morocco was built in 1072 or 1073 by the famous Yousel-Ben-Tashfin, King of Samtuna, and of the dynasty of the Almoravedi, or Marabouts. Its site is that of an ancient city, Martok, founded in the remotest periods of the primitive Africans, or aboriginal Berbers, in whose language it signifies a place where everything good and pleasant was to be found in abundance.

Bocanum Hermerum of the Ancients was also near the site of this capital, Morocco attained its greatest prosperity shortly after its foundation, and since then it has only declined. In the twelfth century, under the reign of Jâkoub Almanzor, there were 10,000 houses and 700,000 souls, (if indeed we can trust their statistics); but, at the present time, there are only some forty to fifty thousand inhabitants, including 4,000 Shelouhs and 5,000 Jews. Ali Bey, in 1804, estimates its population at only 30,000, and Captain Washington in 1830 at 80, or 100,000. This vast city lies at the foot of the Atlas, or about fourteen miles distant, spread over a wide and most lovely plain of the province of Rhamma, watered by the river Tensift, six miles from the gates of the capital.

The mosques are numerous and rich, the principal of which are El-Kirtubeeah, of elegant architecture with an extremely lofty minaret; El-Maazin, which is three hundred years old, and a magnificent building; and Benious, built nearly seven hundred years ago of singular construction, uniting modern and ancient architecture. The mosque of the patron saint is Sidi Belabbess. Nine gates open in the city-walls; these are strong and high, and flanked with towers, except on the south east where the Sultan's palace stands. The streets are crooked, of uneven width, unpaved, and dirty in winter, and full of dust in summer.

There are several public squares and market-places. The Kaessaria, or commercial quarter, is extensive, exhibiting every species of manufacture and natural product.

The manufactures of this, as of other large places, are principally, silks, embroidery, and leather. The merchants of Mogador have magazines here; this capital has also its caravans, which trade to the interior, passing through Wadnoun to the south.

The Imperial palace is without the city and fortified with strong walls. There are large gardens attached, in one of which the Emperor receives his merchants and the diplomatic agents. The air of the country, at the foot of the Atlas, is pure and salubrious. The city is well supplied with water from an aqueduct, connecting it with the river Tensift, which flows from the gorges of the Atlas. But the inhabitants, although they enjoy this inestimable blessing in an African climate, are not famous for their cleanliness; Morocco, if possessing any particular character, still must be considered as a commercial city, for its learning is at a very low ebb. Its interior wears a deeply dejected, nay a profoundly gloomy aspect.

"Horrendum incultumque specus."

and the European merchants, when they come up here are glad to get away as soon as possible.

Outside the city, there is a suburb appropriated to lepers, a Lazar-house of leprosy, which afflicting and loathsome disease descends from father to son through unbroken generations; the afflicted cannot enter the city, and no one dare approach their habitations. The Emperor usually resides for a third portion of his time at Morocco the rest at Fez and Mequinez. Whenever his Imperial Highness has anything disagreeable with foreign European powers, he comes down from Fez to Morocco, to get out of the way. Occasionally, he travels from town to town of the interior, to awe by his presence the ever restless disaffection of the tribes, or excite their loyalty for the Shereefian throne.

Morocco is placed in Lat. 31° 37" 31" N. and Long. 7° 35" 30', W.

Tafilett consists of a group of towns or villages, situate on the south-eastern side of the Atlas, which may be added to the royal cities, being inhabited in part by the Imperial family, and is the birth-place of their sovereign power

—emphatically called Beladesh-Sherfa, " country of the Shereefs." The country was anciently called Sedjelmasa, and retained this name up to 1530 A.D., when the principal city acquired the apellation of Tafilett, said to be derived from an Arab immigrant, called Filal, who improved the culture of dates, and whose name on this account, under the Berber form of Tafilett, was given to a plantation of dates cultivated by him, and then passed to the surrounding districts.

At the present time, Tafilett consists of a group of fortified or castle-built villages, environed by walls mounted with square towers, which extend on both sides of the river Zig. There is also a castle, or rather small town, upon the left side of the river, called by the ordinary name of Kesar, which is in the hands of the Shereefs, and inhabited entirely by the family of the Prophet. The principal and most flourishing place was a long time called Tafilett, but is now according to Callié, Ghourlan, and the residence of the Governor of the province of Ressant, a town distinguished by a magnificent gateway surrounded with various coloured Dutch tiles, symmetrically arranged in a diamond pattern. This traveller calls the district of Tafilett, Afile or Afilel.

It is probable that from the ruins of the ancient Sedjelmasa, some of the modern villages have been constructed. The towns and districts of Tafilett once formed an independent kingdom. The present population has been estimated at some ten thousand, but this is entirely conjectural. Callié mentions the four towns of Ghourlan, L'Eksebi, Sosso and Boheim as containing eleven or twelve thousand souls. The soil of Tafilett is level, composed of sand of an ashy grey, productive of corn, and all sorts of European fruits and vegetables. The natives have fine sheep, with remarkably white wool. The manufactures, which are in woollen and silk, are called Tafiletes.

Besides being a rendezvous of caravans, radiating through all parts of the Sahara, Tafilett is a great mart of traffic in the natural products of the surrounding countries. A fine bridge spans the Zig, built by a Spaniard. When the Sultan of Morocco finds any portion of his family inclined to be naughty, he sends them to Tafilett, as we are wont to send troublesome people to "Jericho." This, at any rate, is better than cutting off their heads, which, from time immemorial, has been the invariable practice of African and Oriental despots. The Maroquine princes may be thankful they have Tafilett as a place of exile. The Emperors never visit Tafilett except as dethroned exiles. A journey to such a place is always attended with danger; and were the Sultan to escape, he would find, on his return, the whole country in revolt.

Regarding these royal cities, we sum up our observations. The destinies of Fez and Mequinez are inseparable. United, they contain one hundred thousand inhabitants, the most polished and learned in the Empire. Fez is the city of arts and learning, that is of what remains of the once famous and profound Moorish doctors of Spain. Mequinez is the strong place of the Empire, an emporium of arms and imperial treasures. Fez is the rival of Morocco. The two cities are the capitals of two kingdoms, never yet amalgamated. The present dynasty belongs not to Fez, but to Morocco; though a dynasty of Shereefs, they are Shereefs of the south, and African blood flows in their veins.

The Sultan generally is obliged to give a preference to Fez for a residence, because his presence is necessary to maintain the allegiance of the north country, and to curb its powerful war-party, his son in the meanwhile being left Governor during his absence. But all these royal cities are on the decline, the " sere and yellow leaf" of a well nigh defunct civilization. Morocco is a huge shell of its former greatness, a monster of Moresque dilapidations. France may awaken the slumbering energies of the population of these once flourishing and august cities, but left to themselves they are powerless, sinking under their own weight and uncouth encumbrances, and will rise no more till reconstructed by European hands.

## CHAPTER VI.

Description of the towns and cities of the Interior, and those of the Kingdom of Fez.—Seisouan.—Wazen.—Zawiat.—Muley Dris.—Sofru.—Dubdu.—Taza.—Oushdah.—Agla.—Nakhila.—Meshra.—Khaluf.—The Places distinguished in Morocco, including Sous, Draha, and Tafilett.—Tefza.—Pitideb.—Ghuer.—Tyijet.—Bulawan.—Soubeit—Meramer.—El-Medina.—Tagodast.—Dimenet.—Aghmat.—Fronga.—Tedmest.—Tekonlet.—Tesegdelt.—Tagawost.—Tedsi Beneali.—Beni Sabih.—Tatta and Akka.—Mesah or Assah.—Talent.—Shtouka.—General observations on the statistics of population.—The Maroquine Sahara.

WE have briefly to notice the remaining towns and cities of the interior, with some other remarkable places.

First, these distinguished and well ascertained places in the kingdom of Fez.

Seisouan, or Sousan, is the capital of the Rif province, situate also on the borders of the province of the Habat, and by the sources of a little river which runs into the Mediterranean, near Cape Mazari. The town is small, but full of artizans and merchants. The country around is fertile, being well irrigated with streams. Sousan is the most beautifully picturesque of all the Atlas range.

Sofou, or Sofron, is a fine walled city, southeast of Fez, situate upon the river Guizo; in a vast and well-watered plain near, are rich mines of fossil salt.

Wazen, or Wazein, in the province of Azgar, and the region of the Gharb, is a small city without walls, celebrated for being the residence of the High Priest, or Grand Marabout of the Empire. This title is hereditary, and is now (or up to lately) possessed by the famous Sidi-el-Haj-el-Araby-Ben-Ali, who, in his district, lives in a state of nearly absolute independence, besides exercising great influence over public affairs. This saint, or priest, has, however, a rival at Tedda. The two popes together pretend to decide the fate of the Empire. The districts where these Grand Marabouts reside, are without governors, and the inhabitants pay no tribute into the imperial coffers, they are ruled by their two priests under a species of theocracy. The Emperor never attempts or dares to contest their privileges. Occasionally they appear abroad, exciting the people, and declaiming against the vices of the times. His Moorish Majesty then feels himself ill at ease, until they retire to their sanctuaries, and employs all his arts to effect the object, protesting that he will be wholly guided by their councils in the future administration of the Empire. With this humiliation of the Shereefs, they are satisfied, and kennel themselves into their sanctum-sanctorums.

Zawiat-Muley-Driss, which means, retirement of our master, Lord Edris (Enoch) and sometimes called Muley Edris, is a far famed city of the province of Fez, and placed at the foot of the lofty mountains of Terhoun, about twenty-eight miles from Fez, north-west, amidst a most beautiful country, producing all the necessaries and luxuries of human life. The site anciently called Tuilet, was perhaps also the Volubilis of the ancients. Here is a sanctuary dedicated to the memory of Edris, progenitor and founder of the dynasty of Edrisiti.

The population, given by Gräberg, is nine thousand, but this is evidently exaggerated. Not far off, towards the west, are some magnificent ruins of an ancient city, called Kesar Farâoun, or " Castle of Pharoah."

Dubdu, called also Doubouton, is an ancient, large city, of the district of Shaous, and once the residence of an independent prince, but now fallen into decay on account of the sterility of its site, which is upon the sides of a barren mountain. Dubdu is three days' journey south-east of Fez, and one day from Taza, in the region of the Mulweeah. Taza is the capital of the well-watered district of Haiaina, and one of the finest cities in Morocco, in a most romantic situation, placed on a rock which is shaped like an island, and in presence of the lofty mountains of Zibel Medghara, to the south-west. Perhaps it is the Babba of the ancients; a river runs round the town. The houses and streets are spacious, and there is a large mosque. The air is pure, and provisions are excellent. The population is estimated at ten or twelve thousand, who are hospitable, and carry on a good deal of commerce with Tlemsen and Fez. Taza is two days from Fez, and four from Oushda.

Oushda is the well-known frontier town, on the north-east, which acquired some celebrity during the late war. It is enclosed by the walls of its gardens, and is protected by a large fortress. The place contains a population of from six hundred to one thousand Moors and Arabs. There is a mosque, as well as three chapels, dedicated to Santous. The houses, built of clay, are low and of a wretched appearance; the streets are winding, and covered with flints. The fortress, where the Kaed resides, is guarded in ordinary times by a dozen soldiers; but, were this force increased, it could not be defended, in consequence of its dilapidated condition. A spring of excellent water, at a little distance from Oushda, keeps up the whole year round freshness and verdure in the gardens, by means of irrigation. Cattle hereabouts is of fine quality. Oushda is a species of oasis of the Desert of Angad, and the aridity of the surrounding country makes these gardens appear delicious, melons, olives, and figs being produced in abundance.

The distance between Tlemsen and Oushda is sixteen leagues, or about sixteen hours' march for troops; Oushda is also four or five days from Oran, and six days from Fez. The Desert commences beyond the Mulweeah, at more than forty leagues from Tlemsen. Like the Algerian Angad, which extends to the south of Tlemsen, it is of frightful sterility, particularly in summer. In this season, one may march for six or eight hours without finding any water. It is impossible to carry on military operations in such a country during summer. On this account, Marshal Bugeaud soon excavated Oushda and returned to the Tlemsen territory.

Aghla is a town, or rather large village, of the district of Fez, where the late Muley Suleiman occasionally resided. It is situated along the river Wad Vergha, in a spacious and well-cultivated district. A great market of cattle, wool, and bees'-wax, is held in the neighbourhood. The country abounds in lions; but, it is pretended, of such a cowardly race, that a child can frighten them away. Hence the proverb addressed to a pusillanimous individual, "You are as brave as the lions of Aghla, whose tails the calves eat." The Arabs certainly do occasionally run after lions with sticks, or throw stones at them, as we are accustomed to throw stones at dogs.

Nakhila, *i.e.*, "little palm," is a little town of the province of Temsna, placed in the river Gueer; very ancient, and formerly rich and thickly populated. A great mart, or souk, is is annually held at this place. It is the site of the ancient Occath.

Meshru Khaluf, *i.e.*, "ford, or watering-place of the wild-boar," in the district of the Beni-Miskeen, is a populated village, and situated on the right bank of the Ovad Omm-Erbergh, lying on the route of many of the chief cities. Here is the ford of Meshra Khaluf, forty-five feet wide, from which the village derives its name.

On the map will be seen many places called Souk. The interior tribes resort thither to purchase and exchange commodities. The market-places form groups of villages. It is not a part of my plan to give any particular description of them.

Second, those places distinguished in the

kingdom of Morocco, including Sous, Draha, and Tafilett.

Tefza, a Berber name, which, according to some, signifies " sand," and to others, " a bundle of straw," is the capital of the province of Todla, built by the aborigines on the slope of the Atlas, who surrounded it with a high wall of sandstone (called, also, Tefza.) At two miles east of this is the smaller town of Efza, which is a species of suburb, divided from Tefza by the river Derna. The latter place is inhabited certainly by Berbers, whose women are famous for their woollen works and weaving. Tefza is also celebrated for its native black and white woollen manufactures. The population of the two places is stated at upwards of 10,000, including 2,000 Jews.

Pitideb, or Sitideb, is another fine town in the neighbourhood, built by the Amazirghs on the top of a high mountain. The inhabitants are esteemed the most civilized of their nation, and governed by their own elders and chiefs, they live in a state of almost republican independence. Some good native manufactures are produced, and a large commerce with strangers is carried on. The women are reputed as being extremely fair and fascinating.

Ghuer, or Gheu, (War, *i.e.*, " difficult ?") is a citadel, or rather a strong, massive rock, and the most inaccessible of all in Morocco, forming a portion of the mountains of Jedla, near the sources of the Wad Omm-Erbegh. This rocky fort is the residence of the supreme Amrgar, or chief of the Amazirghs, who rendered himself renowned through the empire by fighting a pitch-battle with the Imperial troops in 1819. Such chiefs and tribes occasion the weakness of the interior; for, whenever the Sultan has been embroiled with European Powers, these aboriginal Amazirghs invariably seized the opportunity of avenging their wrongs and ancient grudges. The Shereefs always compound with them, if they can, these primitive tribes being so many centres of an *imperium imperio,* or of revolt and disaffection.

Tijijet in the province of Dukkalah, situate on the left bank of the river Omm-Erbegh, along the route from Fez to Morocco, is a small town, but was formerly of considerable importance.

A famous market for grain is held here, which is attended by the tribe of the Atlas: the country abounds in grain and cattle of the finest breed.

Bulawan or Bou-el-Awan, " father of commodious ways or journeys," is a small town of 300 houses, with an old castle, formerly a place of consequence; and lying on an arm of the river Omm-Erbegh *en route* from Morocco to Salee and Mequinez and commanding the passage of the river. It is 80 miles from Morocco, and 110 from Salee. On the opposite side of the river, is the village of Taboulaunt, peopled mostly with Jews and ferrymen.

Soubeit is a very ancient city on the left

bank of the Omm-Erbegh, surrounded with walls, and situate twenty miles from El-Medina in a mountainous region abounding with hares; it is inhabited by a tribe of the same name, or probably Sbeita, which is also the name of a tribe south of Tangier.

Meramer is a city built by the Goths on a fertile plain, near Mount Beni-Megher, about fourteen miles east of Saffee, in the province of Dukkala, and carrying on a great commerce in oil and grain.

El-Medina is a large walled populous city of merchants and artizans, and capital of the district of Haskowra; the men are seditious, turbulent and inhospitable; the women are reputed to be fair and pretty, but disposed, when opportunity offers, to confer their favours on strangers.

There is another place four miles distant of nearly the same name.

Tagodast is another equally large and rich city of the province of Haskowra crowning the heights of a lofty mountain surrounded by four other mountains, but near a plain of six miles in extent, covered with rich vegetation producing an immense quantity of Argan oil, and the finest fruits.

This place contains about 7,000 inhabitants, who are a noble and hospitable race. Besides, Argan oil, Tagodast is celebrated for its red grapes, which are said to be as large as hen's eggs—the honey of Tagodast is the finest in Africa. The inhabitants trade mostly with the south.

Dimenet or Demnet is a considerable town, almost entirely populated by the Shelouhs and Caraaite Jews; it is situate upon the slopes of a mountain of the same name, or Adimmei, in the district of Damnat, fifteen miles distant from Wad Tescout, which falls into the Tensift. The inhabitants are reputed to be of a bad and malignant character, but, nevertheless, learned in Mussulman theology, and fond of disputing with foreigners. Orthodoxy and morality are frequently enemies of one another, whilst good-hearted and honest people are often hetherodox in their opinions.

Aghmat, formerly a great and flourishing city and capital of the province of Rhamna, built by the Berbers, and well fortified—is now fallen into decay, and consists only of a miserable village inhabited by some sixty families, among which are a few Jews—Aghmat lies at the foot of Mount Atlas, on the road which conducts to Tafilett, near a river of the same name, and in the midst of a fine country abounding in orchards and vine-yards; Aghmat was the first capital of the Marabout dynasty.

Fronga is a town densely populated almost entirely by Shelouhs and Jews, lying about fifteen miles from the Atlas range upon an immense plain which produces the finest grain in Morocco.

Tednest, the ancient capital of the province of Shedmah, and built by the Berbers, is deliciously placed upon a paridisical plain, and was once the residence of the Shereefs. It contains a population of four thousand souls, one thousand eight hundred being Jews occupied with commerce, whilst the rest cultivate the land. This is a division of labour amongst Mahometans and Israelites not unfrequent in North Africa. But, as in Europe, the Jew is the trader, not the husbandman.

Tekoulet is a small and pretty town, rising a short distance from the sea, by the mouth of the stream Dwira, in the province of Hhaha. The water is reckoned the best in the province, and the people are honest and friendly; the Jews inhabit one hundred houses.

Tesegdelt, is another city of the province of Hhaha, very large and rich, perched high upon a mountain, and that fortified by nature. The principal mosque is one of the finest in the empire.

Tagawost is a city, perhaps the most ancient, and indeed the largest of the province of Sous. It is distant ten miles from the great river Sous, and fifty from the Atlas. The suburbs are surrounded with huge blocks of stone. Tegawost contains a number of shops and manufactories of good workmen, who are divided into three distinct classes of people, all engaged in continual hostilities with one another. The men are, however, honest and laborious, while the women are pretty and coquettish. People believe St. Augustine, whom the Mahometans have dubbed a Marabout, was born in this city. Their trade is with the Sahara and Timbuctoo.

Fedsi is another considerable city, anciently the capital of Sous, reclining upon a large arm of the river Sous, amidst a fruitful soil, and contains about fourteen thousand inhabitants, who are governed by republican institutions. It is twenty miles E.N.E. of Taroudant.

Beneali is a town placed near to the source of the river Draha, in the Atlas. It is the residence of the chief of the Berbers of Hadrar, on the southern Atlas.

Beni-Sabih, Moussabal, or Draha, is the

capital of the province of Draha, and a small place, but populated and commercial. On the river of the same name, was the Draha of ancient geography.

Tatta and Akka, are two towns or villages of the province of Draha, situate on the southern confines of Morocco, and points of rendezvous for the caravans in their route over the Great Desert.

Tatta is four days direct east from Akka, and placed in 28° 3′ lat. and 90° 20′ long. west of Paris. Akka consists of two hundred houses, inhabited by Mussulmen, and fifty by Jews. The environs are highly cultivated. Akka is two days east of Wadnoun, situate on a plain at the foot of Gibel-Tizintit, and is placed in 28° 3′ lat. and 10° 51′ long. west of Paris.

Messah, or Assah. Messa is, according to Gräberg, a walled city, built by the Berbers, not far from the river Sous, and divided like nearly all the cities of Sous, into three parts, or quarters, each inhabited by respective classes of Shelouhs, Moors, and Jews. Cities are also divided in this manner in the provinces of Guzzala and Draha. The sea on the coast of Sous throws up a very fine quantity of amber. Male whales are occasionally visitors here. The population is three thousand, but Mr. Davidson's account differs materially. The town is named Assah, and distant about two miles from the sea, there being a few scattered houses on each side of the river, to within half a mile of the sea. The place is of no importance, famed only for having near it a market on Tuesday, to which many people resort. The population may be one hundred. Assah is also the name of the district though which the Sous river flows. The Bas-el-wad (or head of the river) is very properly the name of the upper part of the river; when passing through Taroudant it takes the name of Sous. Fifteen miles from Assah is the town of Aghoulon, containing about six hundred people.

Talent, or Tilin, the difference only is the adding of the Berber termination. The other consonants are the same, perhaps, as Mr. Davidson incidentally mentions. It is a strong city, and capital of the province of Sous-el-Aksa, or the extreme part of Sous. This province is sometimes called Tesset, or Tissert. A portion of it is also denominated Blad-Sidi-Hasham, and forms a free and quasi-independant state, founded in 1810 by the Emir Hasham, son of the Shereef Ahmed Ben Mousa. This prince was the bug-bear of Captain Riley. The district contains upwards of twenty-five thousand Shelouhs and industrious Arabs. Talent is the residence of the prince, and is situate on the declivity of a hill, not far from the river Wad-el-Mesah, or Messa, and a mile from Ilekh, or Ilirgh, a populous village, where there is a famous sanctuary, resorted to by the Mahometans of the surrounding regions, of the name of Sidi Hamed-ou-Mousa, (probably Ben Mousa). The singularity of this sacred village is, that Jews constitute the majority of the population. But they seem absolutely necessary to the very existence of the Mussulmen of North Africa, who cannot live without them, or make profitable exchange of the products of the soil, or of native industry, for European articles of use and luxury.

Shtouka, or Stuka, is, according to some, a large town or village; or, as stated by Davidson, a *district*. The fact is, many African districts are called by the name of a principal town or village in them, and *vice versâ*. This place stands on the banks of the Wad-el-Mesah, and is inhabited by some fifteen hundred Shelouhs, who are governed by a Sheikh, nearly independent of Morocco.

On Talent and Shtouka, Mr. Davidson remarks. " There is no town called Stuka; it is a district; none that I can find called Talent; there is Tilin. The Mesah flows through Stuka, in which district are twenty settlements, or rather towns, some of which are large. They are known in general by the names of the Sheikhs who inhabit them. I stopped at Sheikh Hamed's. Tilin was distant from this spot a day's journey in the mountains towards the source of the river. If by Talent, Tissert is meant, Oferen (a town) is distant six miles.

On the province of Sous generally, Don J. A. Conde has this note:—

"In this region (Sous) near the sea, is the temple erected in honour of the prophet Jonas; it was there he was cast out of the belly of the whale. This temple, says Assed Ifriki, is made of the bones of whales which perish on this coast. A little further on, he alludes to the breaking of horses, and being skilful in bodily exercises, for the Moors and Numidians have always been renowned in that respect.

In the lesser and more remote towns, I have followed generally the enumeration of Count Gräberg, but there are many other places on the maps, with varieties of names or differences of position. Our geography of the interior of

Morocco, especially in the South, is still very obscure, and I have only selected those towns and places of whose present existence there is no question. My object, in the above enumeration, has been simply to give the reader a proximate estimate of the population and resources of this country. Of the strength and number of the tribes of the interior, we know scarcely anything. The names of the towns and villages of the South, so frequently beginning and ending with T., sufficiently indicate the preponderance of the Berber population, under the names of Shelouh or Amazirgh, whilst the great error of writers has been to represent the Arabs as more numerous than this aboriginal population.

Monsieur E. Renou, in his geographical description of the Empire of Morocco (Vol. VIII. of the "Exploration Scientifique," &c.) foolishly observes that there is no way of arriving at correct statistics of this empire, except by comparing it with Algeria; and then remarks, which is true enough, "Malheureusement, la population de l'Algérie n'est pas encore bien connue." When, however, he asserts that the numbers of population given by Jackson and Gräberg are gross, and almost unpardonable exaggerations, given at hazard, I am obliged to agree with him from the personal experience I had in Morocco, and these Barbary countries generally.

Jackson makes the whole of the population to amount to almost fifteen millions, or nearly two thirds more than it probably amounts to. Gräberg estimates it at eight millions and a half. But how, or why, or wherefore, such estimates are made is not so easy to determine. Certain it is, that the whole number of cities which I have enumerated, scarcely represent one million of inhabitants. But for those who like to see something more definite in statistics, however exaggerated may be the estimate, I shall give the more moderate calculations of Gräberg, those of Jackson being beyond all rhyme or reason. Gräberg thus classifies and estimates the population.

| | |
|---|---:|
| Amazirghs, Berbers, and Touaricks. | 2,300,000 |
| Amazirghs, Shelouhs and Arabs | 1,450,000 |
| Arabs, mixed Moors, &c. | 3,550,000 |
| Arabs pure, Bedouins, &c. | 740,000 |
| Israelites, Rabbinists, and Caraites | 339,500 |
| Negroes, Fullans, and Mandingoes | 120,000 |
| Europeans and Christians | 300 |
| Renegades | 200 |
| Total | 8,500,000 |

If two millions are deducted from this amount, perhaps the reader will have something like a probable estimate of the population of Morocco. It is hardly correct to classify Moors as mixed Arabs, many of them being simply descendants of the aboriginal Amazirghs. I am quite sure there are no Touaricks in the Empire of Morocco.

Of the Maroquine Sahara, I have only space to mention the interesting cluster of oases of Figheegh, or Figuiq. Shaw mentions them as "a knot of villagers," noted for their plantations of palm-trees, supplying the western province of Algeria with dates. We have now more ample information of Figheegh, finding this Saharan district to consist of an agglomeration of twelve villages, the more considerable of which are Maiz, counting eight hundred houses, El-Wadghir five hundred, and Zenega twelve hundred. The others vary from one or two hundred houses. The villages are more or less connected together, never farther apart than a quarter of a league, and placed on the descent of Wal-el-Khalouf ("river of the wild boar") whence water is procured for the gardens, containing varieties of fruit-trees and abundance of date-palms, all hedged round with prickly-pears. Madder-root and tobacco are also cultivated, besides barley sufficent for consumption. The wheat is brought from the Teli. The Wad-el-Khalouf is dry, except in winter, but its bed is bored with inexhaustible wells, whose waters are distributed among the gardens by means of a *clepsydra*, or a vessel which drops so much water in an hour. The ancients measured time by the dropping of water, like the falling of sand in the hour-glass.

Some of the houses in these villages have two stories, and are well built; each place has its mosque, its school, its kady, and its sheikh, and the whole agglomeration of oases is governed by a Sheikh Kebir, appointed by the Sultan of Morocco. These Saharan villages are eternally in strife with one another, and sometimes take up arms. On this account, they are surrounded by crenated walls, defended by towers solidly built. The immediate cause of discord here is water, that precious element of all life in the desert. But the imaginations of the people are not satisfied with this simple reason, and they are right, for the cause lies deeply in the human heart. They say, however, their ancestors were cursed by a Marabout, to punish them for their laxity in religion, and this was his anathema, "God make you, until the day of judgment, like wool-comber's cards, the one gnawing the other!"

Their wars, in fact, are most cruel, for they destroy the noble and fruitful palms, which, by a tacit convention, are spared in other parts of the Sahara when these quarrels proceed to bloodshed. They have, besides, great tact in mining, and their reputation as miners has been a long time established. But, happily, they are addicted to commerce and various branches of industry, as well as war, having commercial relations with Fez, Tafilett and Touat, and the people are, therefore, generally prosperous.

## CHAPTER VII.

London Jew-boys.—Excursion to the Emperor's garden, and the Argan Forests.—Another interview with the Governor of Mogador on the Anti-Slavery Address.—Opinion of the Moors on the Abolition of Slavery.

We have at times imported into Mogador a stray London Jew or so, of the lower lemon-selling sort. These lads from the Minories, are highly exasperated against the Moors for treating them with so much contempt. Indeed, a high-spirited London Jew-boy will not stop at Mogador, though the adult merchant will, to get money, for mankind often learn baseness with age, and pass to it through a golden door. One of these Jew-boys, being cursed by a man, naturally cursed him again, "an eye for an eye, a tooth for a tooth." Mr. Willshire did not think so; and, on the complaint of the Moor, the British Consul threw the British Jew-boy into a Moorish prison, where he remained for some days. This is one more instance of the disadvantage of having commercial consuls, where everything is sacrificed to keep on good terms with government authorities.

A fire happened the other night, breaking out in the house of one of the rich Jewish merchants; but it was soon extinguished, the houses being built chiefly of mortar and stone, with very little wood. The Governor got up, and went to the scene of "conflagration;" he cracked a few jokes with the people and went home to bed. The Moors were sorry the fire did not extend itself, wanting to have an opportunity of appropriating a few of the merchant's goods.

I accompanied Mr. and Mrs. Elton, with other friends, to spend the day in the pleasant valley of the Saneeates-Sultan, (Garden of the Emperor) sometimes called Gharset-es-Sultan, three or four hours' ride south from Mogador. The small river of Wad-el-Kesab, (overlooked by the village of Deeabat, where watch-dogs were barking apparently all day long as well as night), lay in our way, and was with difficulty forded, heavy rain having fallen up the country, though none on the coast. These Barbary streams are very deceptive, illustrating the metaphor of the book of Job, " deceitful as a book." To-day, their beds are perfectly dry; to-morrow, a sheet of turbid water dashing and foaming to the ocean, covers them and the country round, whilst the immediate cause is concealed. Abrupt and sudden overflowings occur in all rivers having their source in mountains. The book of Job may also refer to the disappointment of Saharan travellers, who, on arriving weary and thirsty, dying for water, at the stream of the Desert, find it dried up, and so perish.

The country in the valley of the Emperor's garden offers nothing remarkable. Bushes of underwood covering sandy mounds, a few palmettos and Argan trees, in which wild doves fluttered and flew about, were all that broke the monotony of a perfect waste. There were no cultivated lands hereabouts, and I was told that a great part of Morocco presents this desolate aspect. We visited, however, the celebrated Argan tree, which the people pretend was planted by the lieutenant of the Prophet, the mighty Okba, who, having spurred his horse in the roaring rebellious surge of the Atlantic, wept and wailed before Heaven that there were no more nations in whose heart to plunge his awful scimitar—so teaching them the mercy of God! Alas! the old hoary tree, with a most peaceful patriarchal look, seemed to belie the honour, stretching out its broad sinewy arm to shelter a hundred people from the darting fires of an African sun. A more noble object of inanimate nature is not to be contemplated than a large and lofty branching tree; in its boughs and leaves, endlessly varying, matted together and intersecting each other, we see the palpable image of infinity. But in the dry and hot climate of Africa, this tree is a luxury which cannot be appreciated in Europe.

We sat under its fresh shade awhile, gazing with security at the bright fires of the sun, radiating over and through all visible nature. To check our enthusiasm, we had strewn at our feet old broken bottles and crockery, the *débris* and classic relics of former visitors, who were equally attentive to creature-comforts as to the grandeur of the Argan monarch of the surrounding forest.

The Emperor's garden contains a well of water and a few fruit-trees, on the trunk of one of which, a fine fig-tree, were carved, in durable bark, the names of European visitors. Among the rest, that of a famous *belle*, whose gallant worshippers had cut her name over all its broad trunk, though they may have failed to cut their own on the plastic and india-rubber tablet of the fair one's heart. This carving on the fig-tree is the sum of all that Europeans have done in Morocco during several ages. We rather adopt Moorish habits, and descend to their animal gratifications than inculcate our own, or the intellectual pleasures of Christian nations. European females brought up in this country, few excepted, adopt with gusto the lascivious dances of the Mooresses; and if this may be said of them, what may we not think of the male class, who frequently throw off all restraint in the indulgence of their passions?

While reposing under the umbrageous shade of the Argan tree, a Moor related to us wondrous sprite and elfin tales of the forests of of these wilds. At one period, the Argan woods were full of enchantresses, who prevented good Mussulmen from saying their prayers, by dancing before them in all their natural charms, to the sounds of melodious and voluptuous music; and if a poor son of the Prophet, perchance, passed this way at the stated times of prayer, he found it impossible to attend to his devotions, being pestered to death by these naughty houries.

On another occasion, when it was high summer and the sun burnt every leaf of the black Argan foliage to a yellow red, and whilst the arid earth opened her mouth in horrid gaps, crystal springs of water were seen to bubble forth from the bowels of the earth, and run in rills among *parterres* of roses and jessamines. The boughs of the Argan tree also suddenly changed into *jereeds* of the date-palm burdened with luscious fruit; but, on weary travellers descending to slake their parching thirst and refresh themselves, they fell headlong into the gaping holes of the ground, and disappeared in the abyss of the dark entrails of the world.

These Argan forests continued under the

fearful ban of the enchantress and wicked jinns, until a holy man was brought from the farthest desert upon the back of a flying camel, who set free the spell-bound wood by tying on each bewitched tree a small piece of cork bark on which was inscribed the sacred name of the Deity. The legends of these haunted Argan forests remind us of the enchanted wood of Tasso, whose enchantment was dissolved by the gallant knight, Rinaldo, and which enabled the Crusaders to procure wood for the machines of war to assault and capture the Holy City. Two quotations will shew the universality and permanence of superstition, begotten of human hopes and fears. Such is the beautiful imagery devoted to superstitious musings, by the illustrious bard:—

> " While, like the rest, the knight expects to hear
> Loud peals of thunder breaking on his ear,
> A dulcet symphony his sense invades,
> Of nymphs, or dryads, warbling through the shades.
> Soft sighs the breeze, soft purls the silver rill,
> The feathered choir the woods with music fill;

The tuneful swan in dying notes complains;
The mourning nightingale repeats her strains,
Timbrels and harps and human voices join,
And in one concert all the sounds combine!"

Then for the streamlets and flowerets—

"Where'er he treads, the earth her tribute pours,
In gushing springs, or voluntary flowers.
Here blooms the lily; there the fragrant rose;
Here spouts a fountain; there a riv'let flows;
From every spray the liquid manna trills,
And honey from the softening bark distills.
Again the strange the pleasing sound he hears,
Of plaints and music mingling in his ears;
Yet naught appears that mortal voice can frame,
Nor harp, nor timbrel, whence the music came."

I had another interview with the Governor on Anti-Slavery subjects. Mr. Treppass accompanied me, and assisted to interpret. His Excellency was very condescending, and even joked about his own slaves, asking me how much I would give him for them. He then continued:—" I am happy to see you before your departure. Whilst you have been here, I have heard nothing of your conduct but what was just and proper. You are a quiet and prudent man,* and I am sorry I could not assist you in your business (abolition). The Sultan will be glad that you and I have not quarrelled, but are friends." I then asked His Excellency if a person were to come direct from our Government, with larger powers and presents, he would have a better chance of success. The Governor replied, "Not the least whatever. You have done all that could have been done. We look at the subject, not the persons. The Sultan will never listen to anybody on this subject. You may cut off his head, but cannot convince him. If all the Christians of the world were to come and take this country, then,

* It is true enough what the governor says about *quietness*, but the novelty of the mission turned the heads of the people, and made a great noise among them. The slave-dealers of Sous vowed vengeance against me, and threatened to "rip open my bowels" if I went down there.

of course, the Mussulmen would yield the question to superior force, to the decree of God, but not till then."

*Myself.*—" How is it, Sidi, that the Bey of Tunis, and the Imaum of Muscat have entered into engagements with Christians for the suppression of slavery, they being Mussulmen?"

*The Governor.*—" I'll tell you; we Mussulmen are as bad as you Christians. We are full of divisions and sects. Some of our people go to one mosque, and will not go to another. They are foolish (*mahboul*). So it is with the subject of slaves. Some are with you, but most are with me. The Bey of Tunis, and the Imaum have a different opinion from us. They think they are right, and we think we are right; but we are as good as they."

*Myself.*—" Sidi, does not the Koran encourage the abolition of slavery, and command it as a duty to all pious Mussulmen?"

*The Governor.*—" No, it does not command it, but those who voluntarily liberate their slaves are therein commended, and have the blessing of God on them."*

Myself.—"Sidi, is it in my power to do anything for you in London?"

The Governor.—"Speak well of me, that is all. Tell your friends I did all I could for you."

I may mention the opinions of the more respectable Moors, as to the mission. They said, "If you had managed your mission well, the Sultan would have received your Address; your Consul is slack; the French Consul is more active, because he is not the Sultan's merchant. Our Sultan must receive every person, even a beggar, because God receives all. You would not have obtained the liberation of our slaves, but the Sultan would have promised you everything. All that emanates from the

* The Sultan's Minister, Ben Oris, addressing our government on the question says, " Whosoever sets any person free God will set his soul free from the fire," (hell), quoting the Koran.

English people is good this we are certain of; but it would have been better had you come with letters from the Bey of Tunis, shewing what had been done in that country." Mr. Treppass is also of the opinion, that a deputation of several persons, accompanied with some presents for the Emperor and his ministers, would have produced a better effect, by making an appearance of shew and authority, suitable to the ideas of the people.* If coming direct from Government, it would have greater weight.

He thinks, besides, there are a good number of Moors who are favourable to abolition. Of the connexion between the east and Morocco, he says, all the Barbary States look up to the Sultan of Constantinople as to a great authority, and during the last few years, an active correspondence, on religious matters, has been carried on between Morocco and Constantinople, chiefly

* A person going to the Emperor without a present, is like a menace at court, for a present corresponds to our "good morning."

through a celebrated doctor of the name of Yousef. If the Turkish Sultan, therefore, would *bond-fide* abolish the slave-markets, I have no doubt this would produce an impression in Morocco favourable to abolition.

During the time I was in Morocco, I distributed some Arabic tracts, translated from the English by Professor Lee of Cambridge, on the abolition of slavery. A few Arabic Bibles and Hebrew New Testaments were also placed at my disposal for circulation by the Societies. I also wrote an Anti-slavery circular to the British merchants of Mogador, on Lord Brougham's Act.

## CHAPTER VIII.

El-Jereed, the Country of Dates.—Its hard soil.—Salt Lake. Its vast extent.—Beautiful Palm-trees.—The Dates, a staple article of Food.—Some Account of the Date-Palm.—Mode of Culture.—Delicious Beverage.—Tapping the Palm.—Meal formed from the Dates.—Baskets made of the Branches of the Tree.—Poetry of the Palm.—Its Irrigation—Palm-Groves.—Collection of Tribute by the "Bey of the Camp."

EL-JEREED, or Belad-el-Jereed, the country of dates, or literally, the country of the palm branches, is a part of the Sahara, or the hot dry country lying in the immediate vicinity of the Great Desert. Its principal features of soil and climate offer nothing different from other portions of the Sahara, or the Saharan regions of Algeria and Morocco. The Belad-el-Jereed, therefore, may be properly called the Tunisian

Sahara. Shaw observes generally of Jereed:—
" This part of the country, and indeed the whole tract of land which lies between the Atlantic and Egypt, is by most of the modern geographers, called Biledulgerid, a name which they seem to have borrowed from Bloid-el-Jeridde, of the Arabians, who merely signify the dry country; though, if we except the Jeridde, a small portion of it which is situate on this side of Lesser Syrtis, and belongs to the Tunisians, all the rest of it is known by no other general name than the Sahara or Sahra, among those Arabs, at least, whom I have conversed with."

Besides the grand natural feature of innumerable lofty and branching palms, whose dark depending slender leaves, are depicted by the Arabian poet as hanging gracefully like the dishevelled ringlets of a beautiful woman in distress, there is the vast salt lake, El-Sibhah, or literally the "salt plain," and called by some modern geographers the Sibhah-el-Soudeeat, or Lake of Marks, from having certain marks made of the trunks of the palm, to assist the caravans in their marches across its monotonous same-like surface.

This vast lake, or salt plain, was divided by the ancients into three parts, and denominated respectively, Palus Tritonis, Palus Pallas, and Palus Libya. The first is derived from the river Triton, which according to Ptolemy and other ancient geographers, is made to pass through this lake in its course to the sea, but which is the present river Ghobs, where it falls into the Mediterranean. The name Pallas is derived from the tradition of Pallas having accompanied Sesostris in his Asiatic expeditions with the Lybian women, and she may have been a native of the Jereed. The lake measures from north-east to south-west about seventy English miles, with a third of the breadth, but it is not one collection of water; there being several dry places, like so many islands, interspersed over its surface, depending however, as to their number and extent upon the season of the year, and upon the quantity of water in the particular season.

"At first, on crossing it," says a tourist, "the grass and bushes become gradually scarcer; then follows a tract of sand, which some way beyond, becomes in parts covered with a thin layer of salt. This, as you advance, is thicker and more united; then we find it a compact and unbroken mass or sheet, which can, however, be penetrated by a sword, or other sharp instrument, and here it was found to be eleven inches in depth; and finally in the centre, it became so hard, deep, and concentrated, as to baffle all attempts at breaking its surface except with a pickaxe. The horse's shoe, in fact, makes no impression upon its stone-like surface."

The salt of the lake is considerably weaker than that of the sea, and not adapted for preserving provisions, though its flavour is very agreeable; it is not exported, nor made in any way an article of commerce.

The Jereed, from the existence in it of a few antiquities, such as pieces of granite and marble, and occasionally a name or a classic inscription, is proved to have been in the possession of the Romans, and undoubtedly of the Carthaginians before them, who could have had no difficulty in holding this flat and exposed country.

The trade and resources of this country consist principally in dates. The quantity exported to other parts of the Regency, as well as to foreign countries, where their fine quality is well known, is in round numbers on an average from three to four thousand quintals per annum. But in Jereed itself, twenty thousand people live six months of the year entirely on dates.

"A great number of poles," says Sir Grenville Temple, " are arranged across the rooms at the height of eight or nine feet from the ground, and from these are suspended rich and large bunches of dates, which compose the winter store of the inhabitants; and in one corner of the room is one or more large earthern jars about six or seven feet high, also filled with dates pressed close together, and at the bottom of the jar is a cock, from which is drawn the juice in the form of a thick luscious syrup. It is scarcely possible to imagine anything more palatable than this ' sweet of sweets.' "

As we are writing of the country of dates, *par excellence*, I must needs give some description of the palm, but it will be understood that the information is Tunisian, or collected in Tunis, and may differ in some respects from details collected in other parts of North Africa. The date-palm abounds in the maritime as well as in the inland districts of North Africa. They are usually propagated from shoots of full grown trees, which if transplanted and taken care of, will yield in six or seven years, whilst those raised immediately from the stone require sixteen years to produce fruit.

The date-palm is male and female, or *diœcious*, and requires communication, otherwise the fruit is dry and insipid. The age of the palm, in its greatest vigour, is about thirty years, according to the Tunisians, after planting, and will continue in vigour for seventy years, bearing anually fifteen or twenty clusters of dates, each of them fifteen or twenty pounds in weight; after this long period, they begin gradually to wither away. But the Saharan Tripolitans will tell you that the date-palm does not attain its age of full vigour till it reaches a hundred years, and then will flourish two or or three centuries before it withers!

The only culture requisite, is to be well watered at the roots once in four or five days, and to have the lower boughs cut off when they begin to droop and wither. Much rain, however, injures the dates, and we know that the countries in which they flourish, are mostly without rain. In many localities in Africa, date-palms can never be watered in the dry season; it is nevertheless observable that generally wherever a palm grows and thrives water may usually be obtained by boring. The sap, or honey of the palm is a delicious and wholesome beverage when drunk quite fresh; but if allowed to remain for some hours, it acquires a sharp taste, something like cider, and becomes very intoxicating. It is called poetically *leghma*, " tears" of the dates. When a tree is found not to produce much fruit, the head is cut off, and a bowl or cavity scooped out of the summit, in which the rising sap is collected, and this is drunk in its pure state without any other preparation. If the tree be not exhausted by draining, in five or six months it grows afresh; and, at the end of two or three years, may again be cut or tapped. The palm is capable of undergoing this operation five or six times, and it may be easily known how often a tree has been cut by the number of rings of a narrow diameter which are seen towards its summit; but, if the sap is allowed to flow too long, it will perish entirely at the end of a year. This sap, by distillation, produces an agreeable spirit called *Aráky* or *Arák:* from the fruit also the Jews distil a spirit called *bokka*, or what we should call *toddy*. It is usual for persons of distinction to entertain their friends upon a marriage, or the birth of a child, with this pure sap, and a tree is usually tapped for the purpose. It would appear that tapping the palm was known to the ancients, for a cornelian *intaglio* of Roman antiquity, has been found in the Jereed, representing a tree in this state, and the jars in which the juice was placed.

Dates are likewise dried in the sun, and reduced into a kind of meal, which will keep for any length of time, and which thus becomes a most valuable resource for travellers crossing the deserts, who frequently make it their only food, moistening a handful of it with a little water. Certain preparations are made of the male plant, to which medicinal virtues are attributed; the younger leaves, eaten with salt, vinegar, and oil, make an excellent salad. The heart of the tree, which lies at top between the fruit branches, and weighs from ten to twenty pounds, is eaten only on grand occasions, as those already mentioned, and possesses a delicious flavour between that of a banana and a pine-apple.

The palm, besides these valuable uses to which it is applied, superseding or supplying the place of all other vegetables to the tribes of the Jereed, is, nevertheless, still useful for a great variety of other purposes. The most beautiful baskets, and a hundred other nicknackery of the wickery sort are made of its branches; ropes are made and vestments wove from the long fibres, and its wood, also, when hardened by age, is used for building. Indeed, we may say, it is the all and everything of the Jereed, and, as it is said of the camel and the desert, *the palm is made for the Jereed, and the Jereed is made for the palm.*

The Mussulmen make out a complete case of piety and superstition in the palm, and pretend that *they are made for the palm, and the palm is made for them,* alleging that, as soon as the Turks conquered Constantinople, the palm raised its graceful flowing head over the domes of the former infidel city, whilst when the Moors evacuated Spain, the palm pined away, and died. "God," adds the pious Mussulman, "has given us the palm; amongst the Christians, it will not grow!" But the poetry of the palm is an inseparable appendage in the North African landscape, and even town-scenery. The Moor and the Arab, whose minds are naturally imbued with the great images of nature, so glowingly represented also in the sacred leaves of the Koran, cannot imagine a mosque or the dome-roof of a hermitage, without the dark leaf of the palm overshadowing it; but the serenest, loveliest object on the face of the landscape is *the lonely palm*, either thrown by chance on the brow of some savage hill, or planted by design to adorn some sacred spot of mother-earth.

I must still give some other information which I have omitted respecting this extraordinary tree. And, after this, I further refer the reader to a Tour in the Jereed of which some details are given in succeeding pages. A palm-grove is really a beautiful object, and requires scarcely less attention than a vineyard. The trees are generally planted in a *quincunx*, or at times without any regular order; but at distances from each other of four or five yards. The situation selected is mostly on the banks of some stream or rivulet, running from the neighbouring hills, and the more abundant the supply of water, the healthier the plants and the finer the fruit. For this tree, which loves a warm climate, and a sandy soil, is yet wonderfully improved by frequent irrigation, and, singularly, the *quality* of the water appears of little consequence, being salt or sweet, or impregnated with nitre, as in the Jereed.

Irrigation is performed in the spring, and through the whole summer. The water is drawn by small channels from the stream to each individual tree, around the stalk and root of which a little basin is made and fenced round with clay, so that the water, when received, is detained there until it soaks into the earth. (All irrigation is, indeed, effected in this way.) As to the abundance of the plantations, the fruit of one plantation alone producing fifteen hundred camels' loads of dates, or four thousand five hundred quintals, three quintals to the load, is not unfrequently sold for one thousand dollars. Besides the Jereed, Tafilett, in Morocco, is a great date-country. Mr. Jackson says, " We found the country covered with most magnificent plantations, and extensive forests of the lofty date, exhibiting the most elegant and picturesque appearance that nature on a plain surface can present to the admiring eye. In these forests, there is no underwood, so that a horseman may gallop through them without impediment."

Our readers will see, when they come to the Tour, that this description of the palm-groves agrees entirely with that of Mr. Reade and Captain Balfour. I have already mentioned that the palm is male and female, or, as botanists say, *diœcious;* the Moors, however, pretend that the palm in this respect is just like the human being. The *female* palm alone produces fruit and is cultivated, but the presence or vicinity of the *male* is required, and in many oriental countries there is a law that those who own a palm-wood must have a certain number of *male* plants in proportion. In Barbary they seem to trust to chance, relying on the male plants which grow wild in the Desert. They hang and shake them over the female plants, usually in February or March. Koempfe says, that the male flowers, if plucked when ripe, and cautiously dried, will even, in this state, perform their office, though kept to the following year.

The Jereed is a very important portion of the Tunisian territory, Government deriving a large revenue from its inhabitants. It is visited every year by the "Bey of the Camp," who administers affairs in this country as a sovereign;

and who, indeed, is heir-apparent to the Tunisian throne. Immediately on the decease of the reigning Bey, the "Bey of the Camp" occupies the hereditary beylick, and nominates his successor to the camp and the throne, usually the eldest of the other members of the royal family, the beylick not being transmitted from father to son, only on the principle of age. At least, this has been the general rule of succession for many years.

The duties of the "Bey of the Camp" is to visit with a "flying-camp," for the purpose of collecting tribute, the two circuits or divisions of the Regency.

I now introduce to the reader the narrative of a Tour to the Jereed, extracted from the note-books of the tourists, together with various observations of my own interspersed, and some additional account of Toser, Nefta, and Ghafsa.

## CHAPTER IX.

Tour in the Jereed of Captain Balfour and Mr. Reade.—Sidi Mohammed.—Plain of Manouba.—Tunis.—Tfeefleeah.—The Bastinado. — Turkish Infantry. — Kairwan. — Sidi Amour Abeda.—Saints.—A French Spy —Administration of Justice.—The Bey's presents.—The Hobara.—Ghafsa. Hot streams containing Fish.—Snakes.—Incantation.—Moorish Village.

The tourists were Captain Balfour, of the 88th Regiment, and Mr. Richard Reade, eldest son of Sir Thomas Reade.

The morning before starting from Tunis they went to the Bardo to pay their respects to Sidi Mohammed, " Bey of the Camp," and to thank him for his condescending kindness in taking them with him to the Jereed. The Bey told him to send their baggage to Giovanni, " Guarda-pipa," which they did in the evening.

At nine A. M. Sidi Mohammed left the Bardo under a salute from the guns, one of the wads of which nearly hit Captain Balfour on the head. The Bey proceeded across the plain of Manouba, mounted on a beautiful bay charger, in front of the colours, towards Beereen, the greater part of the troops of the expedition following, whilst the entire plain was covered with baggage-camels, horses, mules, and detached parties of attendants, in glorious confusion.

The force of the camp consisted of—
Mamelukes of the Seraglio, superbly mounted . . . 20
Mamelukes of the Skeefah, or those who guard the entrance of the Bey's palace, or tent, and are all Levantines . . . 20
Boabs, another sort of guard of the Bey, who are always about the Bey's tent, and must be of this country 20

| | |
|---|---:|
| Turkish Infantry | 300 |
| Spahis, o. mounted Arab guards | 300 |
| Camp followers (Arabs) | 2,000 |
| Total | 2,660 |

This is certainly not a large force, but in several places of the march they were joined for a short time by additional Arab troops, a sort of honorary welcome for the Bey. As they proceeded, the force of the camp-followers increased; but, in returning, it gradually decreased, the parties going home to their respective tribes. We may notice the total absence of any of the new corps, the Nithàm. This may have been to avoid exciting the prejudices of the people; however, the smallness of the force shows that the districts of the Jereed are well-affected. The summer camp to Beja has a somewhat larger force, the Arabs of that and other neighbouring districts not being so loyal to the Government.

Besides the above-named troops, there were two pieces of artillery. The band attendant on these troops consisted of two or three flageolets, kettle-drums, and trumpets made of cow-horns, which, according to the report of our tourists, when in full play produced the most diabolical discord.

After a ride of about three hours, we pitched our tents at Beereen. Through the whole of the route we marched on an average of about four miles per hour, the horses, camels, &c., walking at a good pace. The Turkish infantry always came up about two hours after the mounted troops. Immediately on the tents being pitched, we went to pay our respects to the Bey, accompanied by Giovanni, "Guarda-pipa," as interpreter. His Highness received us very affably, and bade us ask for anything we wanted. Afterwards, we took some luncheon with the Bey's doctor, Signore Nunez Vaise, a Tuscan Jew, of whose kindness during our whole tour it is impossible to speak too highly. The doctor had with him an assistant, and tent to himself. Haj Kador, Sidi Shakeer, and several other Moors, were of our luncheon-party, which was a very merry one.

About half-way to Beereen, the Bey stopped at a marabet, a small square white house, with a dome roof, to pay his devotions to a great Marabout, or saint, and to ask his parting blessing on the expedition. They told us to go on, and joined us soon after. Two hours after us, the Turkish Agha arrived, accompanied with colours, music, and some thirty men. The Bey received the venerable old gentleman under an immense tent in the shape of an umbrella, surrounded with his mamelukes and officers of state. After their meeting and saluting, three guns were fired. The Agha was saluted every day in the same manner, as he came up with his infantry after us. We retired for the night at about eight o'clock.

The form of the whole camp, when pitched, consisting of about a dozen very large tents, was as follows :—The Bey's tent in the centre, which was surrounded at a distance of about forty feet with those of the Bash-Hamba* of the Arabs, the Agha of the Arabs, the Sahab-el-Tabah, Haznadar or treasurer, the Bash-Boab, and that of the English tourists; then further off were the tents of the Katibs and Bash-Katib, the Bash-Hamba of the Turks, the doctors, and the domestics of the Bey, with the cookery establishment. Among the attendants of the Bey were the "guarda-pipa," guard of the pipe, "guarda-fusile," guard of the gun, "guarda-cafè," guard of the coffee, "guarda-scarpe," guard of the shoes,† and "guarda-acqua," guard of water. A man followed the Bey about holding in his hand a golden cup, and leading a mule, having two paniers on its back full of water, which was brought from Tunis by camels. There was also a story-teller, who entertained the Bey every night with the most extraordinary stories, some

---

\* *Bash*, means chief, as Bash-Mameluke, chief of the Mamelukes. It is a Turkish term.

† This office answers vulgarly to our *Boots* at English inns.

of them frightfully absurd. The Bey did not smoke—a thing extraordinary, as nearly all men smoke in Tunis. His Highness always dined alone. None of his ladies ever accompany him in these expeditions.

The tents had in them from twenty to fifty men each. Our tent consisted of our two selves, a Boab to guard the baggage, two Arabs to tend the horses and camels, and another Moor of all work, besides Captain Balfour's Maltese, called Michael. We had three camels for our baggage. The first night we found very cold; but having abundance of clothing, we slept soundly, in spite of the perpetual wild shoutings of the Arab sentries, stationed round the camp, the roaring and grumbling of the camels, the neighing and coughing of the horses, all doing their utmost to drive away slumber from our eyelids.

We halted on the morrow, which gave us an opportunity of getting a few things from Tunis which we had neglected to bring. But before returning, we ate some sweetmeats sent us by the guarda-pipa, with a cup of coffee. The guarda-pipa is also a dragoman interpreter of his Highness, and a Genoese by birth, but now a renegade. In this country they do not know what a good breakfast is; they take a cup of coffee in the morning early, and wait till twelve or one o'clock, when they take a hearty meal, and then sup in the evening, late or early, according to the season. Before returning to Tunis, we called upon his Highness, and told him our object. We afterwards called to see the Bey every morning, to pay our respects to him, as was befitting on these occasions. His Highness entered into the most familiar conversation with us.

On coming back again from Tunis, it rained hard, which continued all night. In the evening the welcome news was proclaimed that the tents would not be struck until daylight: previously, the camp was always struck at 3 o'clock, about three hours before daylight, which gave rise to great confusion, besides being without shelter during the coldest part of the night (three hours before sun-rise) was a very serious trial for the health of the men. The reason, however, was, to enable the camels to get up to the new encampment; their progress, though regular and continual, is very slow.

Of a morning the music played off the *réveil* an hour before sunrise. The camp presented an animated appearance, with the striking of tents, packing camels, mounting horses, &c. We paid our respects to his Highness, who was sitting in an Arab tent, his own being down. The music was incessantly grating upon our ears, but was in harmony with the irregular marching and movements of the Arabs, one of them occasionally rushing out of the line of march, charging, wheeling about, firing, reloading, shouting furiously, and making the air ring with his cries.

The order of march was as follows:—The Bey mounts, and, going along about one hundred yards from the spot, he salutes the Arab guards, who follow behind him; then, about five or six miles further, overtaking the Turkish soldiers, who, on his coming up, are drawn up on each side of the road, his Highness salutes them; and then afterwards the water-carriers are saluted, being most important personages in the dry countries of this circuit, and last of all, the gunners; after all which, the Bey sends forward a mameluke, who returns with the Commander, or Agha of the Arabs, to his Highness. This done, the Bey gallops off to the right or left from the line of march, on whichsoever side is most game—the Bey going every day to shoot, whilst the Agha takes his place and marches to the next halting-place.

One morning the Bey shot two partridges while on horseback. "In fact," says Mr. Rade, "he is the best shot on horseback I ever saw—he seldom missed his game." As Captain B. was riding along with the doctor, they remarked a cannon-ball among some ruins;

but, being told a saint was buried there, they got out of the way as quick as if a deadly serpent had been discovered. Stretching away to the left, we saw a portion of the remains of the Carthaginian aqueduct. The march was only from six to eight miles, and the encampment at Tfeefleeah. At day-break, at noon, at 3 o'clock, P.M. and at sunset, the Muezzen called from outside and near the door of the Bey's tent the hour of prayer. An aide-de-camp also proclaimed, at the same place, whether we should halt, or march, on the morrow. The Arabs consider fat dogs a great delicacy, and kill and eat them whenever they can lay hands upon them. Captain B. was fortunate in not bringing his fat pointer, otherwise he would have lost him. The Arabs eat also foxes and wolves, and many animals of the chase not partaken of by us. The French in Algiers kill all the fat cats, and turn them into hares by dexterous cooking. The mornings and evenings we found cold, but mid-day very hot and sultry.

We left Tfeefleeah early, and went in search of wild-boar; found only their tracks, but saw plenty of partridges and hares; the ground being covered with brushwood and heath, we soon lost sight of them. The Arabs were seen on a sudden running and galloping in all directions, shouting and pointing to a hill, when a huge beast was put up, bristling and bellowing, which turned out to be a hyæna. He was shot by a mameluke, Si Smyle, and fell in a thicket, wallowing in his blood. He was a fine fellow, and had an immense head, like a bull-dog. They put him on a mule, and carried him in triumph to the Bey. When R. arrived at the camp, the Bey sent him the skin and the head as a present, begging that he would not eat the brain. There is a superstitious belief among the Moors that, if a person eats the brain of a hyæna he immediately becomes mad. The hyæna is not the savage beast commonly represented; he rarely attacks any person, and becomes untameably ferocious by being only chained up. He is principally remarkable for his stupidity when at large in the woods. The animal abounds in the forests of the Morocco Atlas. Our tourists saw no lions *en route,* or in the Jereed; the lion does not like the sandy and open country of the plain. Very thick brushwood, and ground broken with rocks, like the ravines of the Atlas, are his haunts.

Several Arabs were flogged for having stolen the barley of which they had charge. The bastinado was inflicted by two inferior mamelukes, standing one on each side of the culprit, who had his hands and his feet tied behind him. In general, it may be said that bastinadoing in Tunis is a matter of form, many of the strokes ordered to be inflicted being never performed, and those given being so many taps or scratches. It is very rare to see a man bleeding from the bastinado; I (the author) never did. It is merely threatened as a terror; whilst it is not to be overlooked, that the soles of the feet of Arabs, and the lower classes in this country, are like iron, from the constant habit of going barefoot upon the sharpest stones. Severe punishments of any kind are rarely inflicted in Tunis.

The country was nearly all flat desert, with scarcely an inhabitant to dissipate its savage appearance. The women of a few Arab horsehair tents (waterproof when in good repair) saluted us as we passed with their shrill loo-loos. There appeared a great want of water. We passed the ruins of several towns and other remains. The camels were always driven into camp at sunset, and hobbled along, their two fore-legs being tied, or one of them being tied up to the knee, by which the poor animals are made to cut a more melancholy figure than with their usual awkward gait and moody character.

We continued our march about ten miles in nearly a southern direction, and encamped at a place called Heelet-el-Gazlen.

One morning shortly after starting, we came to a small stream with very high and precipitous banks, over which one arch of a fine bridge remained, but the other being wanting, we had to make a considerable *détour* before we could cross; the carriages had still greater difficulty. Here we have an almost inexcusable instance of the disinclination of the Moors to repairs, for had the stream been swollen, the camp would have been obliged to make a round-about march by the way of Hamman-el-Enf, of some thirty miles; and all for the want of an arch which would scarcely cost a thousand piastres! This stream or river is the same as that which passes near Hamman-el-Enf, and the extensive plain through which it meanders is well cultivated, with douwars, or circular villages of the Arabs dotted about. We saw hares, but, the ground being difficult running for the dogs, we caught but few. Bevies of partridges got up, but we were unprepared for them. In the evening, the Bey sent a present of a very fine bay horse to R. Marched about ten miles, and halted at Ben Sayden.

The following day after starting, we left the line of march to shoot; saw one boar, plenty of foxes and wolves, and we put up another hyæna, but the bag consisted principally of partridges, the red-legged partridge or *perdix ruffa*, killed by the Bey, who is a dead-shot. Our ride lay among hills; there was very little water, which accounted for the few inhabitants. After dinner, went out shooting near Jebanah, and bagged a few partridges, but, not returning before the sun went down, the Bey sent a dozen fellows bawling out our names, fearing some harm had befallen us.

On leaving the hills, there lay stretched at our feet a boundless plain, on which is situate Kairwan, extending also to Susa, and leagues around. North Africa, is a country of hills and plains—such was the case along our entire route. We saw a large herd of gazelles feeding, as well as several single ones, but they have the speed of the greyhound, so we did not grace our supper with any. Saw several birds called

Kader, about the size of a partridge, but we shot none. A good many hares and partridges either crossed our path or whirred over our heads. Passed over a running stream called Zebharah, where we saw the remains of an ancient bridge, but in the place where the baggage went over there was a fine one in good repair. Here was a small dome-topped chapel, called Sidi Farhat, in which are laid the ashes of a saint. We had seen many such in the hills; indeed these gubbah abound all over Barbary, and are placed more frequently on elevations. We noticed particularly the 300 Turkish infantry; they were irregulars with a vengeance, though regulars compared to the Arabs. On overtaking them, they drew up on each side, and some dozen of them kept up a running sham fight with their swords and small wooden and metal shields before the Bey. The officers kissed the hand of the Bey, and his treasurer tipped their band, for so we must call their tumtums and squeaking-pipes. This ceremony took place every morning, and they were received in the camp with all the honours. They kept guard during the night, and did all they could to keep us awake by their eternal cry of " Alleya," which means, " Be off," or " Keep your distance !" These troops had not been recruited for eight years, and will soon die off; and yet we see that the Bey treats these remnants of the once formidable Turkish Tunisian Janissaries with great respect; of course, in an affair with the Arabs, their fidelity to the Bey would be most unshaken.

As we journeyed onward, we saw much less vegetation and very little cultivation. An immense plain lay before and around us, in which, however, there was some undulating ground. Passed a good stone bridge; were supplied with water near a large Arab encampment, around which were many droves of camels; turned up several hares, partridges, and gazelles. One of the last gave us a good chase, but the greyhounds caught him; in the first half mile, he certainly beat them by a good half of the instance, but having taken a turn which enabled the dogs to make a short cut, and being blown, they pulled the swift delicate creature savagely down. There were several good courses after hares, though her pursuers gave puss no fair play, firing at her before the dogs and heading her in every possible way.

Rode to Kairwan. Few Christians arrive in this city. Prince Pückler Muskau was the fourth when he visited it in 1835. The town is clean, but many houses are in ruins. The greater part of a regiment of the Nitham are quartered here. The famous mosque, of course, we were not allowed to enter, but many of its marble pillars and other ornaments, we heard from Giovanni, were the spoils of Christian churches and Pagan temples. The house of the Kaëd was a good specimen of dwellings in this country. Going along a street, we were greatly surprised at seeing our attendants, among whom were Si Smyle (a very intelligent and learned man, and who taught Mr. R. Arabic during the tour) and the Bash-Boab, jumping off their horses, and, running up to an old-looking Moor, and then seizing his hand, kissed it; and for some time they would not leave the ragged ruffian-like saint.

At last, having joined us, they said he was Sidi Amour Abeda, a man of exceeding sanctity, and that if the Bey had met the saint, his Highness must have done the same. The saint accompanied us to the Kaëd's house; and, on entering, we saw the old Kaëd himself, who was ill and weeping on account of the arrival of his son, the commander of a portion of the guards of the camp. We went up stairs, and sat down to some sweetmeats which had been prepared for us, together with Si Smyle and Hamda, but, as we were commencing, the saint, who was present, laid hold of the sweets with his hands, and blessed them, mumbling *bismillas*\* and other jargon. We afterwards saw a

---

\* Bismilla, Arabic for "In the name of God!" the Mohammedan grace before meat, and also drink.

little house, in course of erection by order of the Bey, where the remains of Sidi Amour Abeda are to be deposited at his death, so that the old gentleman can have the pleasure of visiting his future burial-place. In this city, a lineal descendant of the Prophet, and a lucky guesser in the way of divining, are the essential ingredients in the composition of a Moorish saint. Saints of one order or another are as thick here as ordinary priests in Malta, whom the late facetious Major Wright was accustomed to call *crows*—from their black dress—but better, cormorants, as agreeing with their habits of fleecing the poor people. Sidi Amour Abeda's hands ought to be lily-white, for every one who meets him kisses them with devout and slavering obeisance. The renegade doctor of the Bey told us that the old dervish now in question would like nothing better than to see us English infidels burnt alive. Fanaticism seems to be the native growth of the human heart!

We afterwards visited the Jabeah, or well,

which they show as a curiosity, as also the camel which turns round the buckets and brings up the water, being all sanctified, like the wells of Mecca, and the drinking of the waters forming an indispensable part of the pilgrimage to all holy Mohammedan cities.

We returned to the Kaëd's, and sat down to a capital dinner. The old Governor was a great fanatic, and when R. ran up to shake hands with him, the mamelukes stopped R. for fear he might be insulted. We visited the fortress, which was in course of repair, our *cicerone* being Sidi Reschid, an artillery-officer. We then returned to the camp, and found Santa Maria, the French officer, had arrived, who, during the tour, employed himself in taking sketches and making scientific observations. He was evidently a French spy on the resources of the Bey. It was given out, however, that he was employed to draw charts of Algiers, Tunis, and Tripoli, by his Government. He endeavoured to make himself as unpopular as some persons try to make themselves agreeable, being very jealous of us, and every little thing that we had he used to cry for it and beg it like a child, sometimes actually going to the Bey's tent in person, and asking his Highness for the things which he saw had been given to us.

We went to see his Highness administer justice, which he always did, morning and evening, whilst at Kairwan. There were many plaintiffs, but no defendants brought up; most of them were turned out in a very summary manner. To some, orders were given, which we supposed enabled them to obtain redress; others were referred to the kadys and chiefs. The Bey, being in want of camels, parties were sent out in search of them, who drove in all the finest that they could find, which were then marked ("tabâ,") *à la Bey*, and immediately became the Bey's property. It was a curious sight to see the poor animals thrown over, and the red-hot iron put to their legs, amidst the cries and curses of their late different owners—all which were not in the least attended to, the wants of the Bey, or Government, being superior on such occasions of necessity, or what not, to all complaint, law, or justice. About two hundred changed hands in this way.

The Bey of Tunis has an immense number of camels which he farms out. He has overseers in certain districts, to whom he gives so many camels; these let them out to other persons for mills and agricultural labours, at so much per head. The overseers annually render an account of them to Government, and, when called upon, supply the number required. At this time, owing to a disorder which had caused a great mortality, camels had been very scarce, and this was the reason of the extensive seizure just mentioned. If an Arab commits manslaughter, his tribe is mulcted thirty-three camels; and, as the crime is rather common in the Bedouin districts, the Bey's acquisition in this way is considerable. A few years ago, a Sicilian nobleman exported from Tunis to Sicily some eighty camels, the duty for which the Bey remitted. The camel, if ever so healthy and thriving in the islands of the Mediterranean, could never supersede the labour of mules. The camel is only useful where there are vast plains to travel, as in North Africa, Arabia, Persia, Australasia, and some parts of the East Indies.

A hundred more Arabs joined, who passed in a single file before the Bey for inspection: they came rushing into the camp by twos and threes, firing off their long guns.

We crossed large plains, over which ran troops of gazelles, and had many gallops after them; but they go much faster than the greyhound, and, unless headed and bullied, there is little chance of taking them, except found asleep. On coming on a troop unawares, R. shot one, which the dogs caught. R. went up afterwards to cut its throat *à la Moresque*, when he was insulted by an Arab. R. noticed the fellow, and afterwards told the Bey, who instantly ordered him to receive two hundred bastinadoes, and to be put in chains; but, just as they had begun to whip him, R. went up and generously begged him off. This is the end of most bastinados in the country. We passed a stream which they said had swallowed up some persons, and was very dangerous. A muddy stream, they add, is often very fatal to travellers. The Bey surprised Captain B. by sending him a handsome black horse as a present; he also sent a grey one to the Frenchman, who, when complaining of it, saying that it was a bad one, to the Bey's mamelukes, his Highness sent for it, and gave him another. Under such circumstances, Saint Mary ought to have looked very foolish. The Bey shot a kader, a handsome bird, rather larger than a partridge, with black wings, and flies like a plover. We had a large hawking-establishment with us, some twenty birds, very fine falconry, which sometimes carried off hares, and even attacked young goat-kids. Marched to a place called Gilma, near which the road passes through an ancient town. Shaw says, " Gilma, the ancient Cilma, or Oppidum Chilmanenense, is six leagues to the east-south-east of Spaitla. We have here the remains of a large city, with the area of a temple, and some other fragments of large buildings. According to the tradition of the Arabs, this place received its name in consequence of a miracle pretended to have been wrought by one of their marabouts, in bringing hither the river of Spaitla, after it was lost underground. For Ja Elma signifies, in their language, 'The water comes!' an expression we are to imagine of surprise at the arrival of the stream."

During our tour, the mornings were generally cold. We proceeded about twenty miles, and encamped near a place called Wady Tuckah. This river comes from the hills about three or four miles off, and when the camp arrives at Kairwan, the Bey sends an order to the Arabs of the district to let the water run down to the place where the tents are pitched. When we arrived, the water had just come. We saw warrens of hares, and caught many with the dogs. Troops of gazelles were also surprised; one was fired at, and went off scampering on three legs. The hawks caught a beautiful bird called hobara, or habary,* about the size of the small hen-turkey, lily white on the back, light brown brindle, tuft of long white

---

* Shaw says: "The hobara is of the bigness of a capon, it feeds upon the little grubs or insects, and frequents the confines of the Desert. The body is of a light dun or yellowish colour, and marked over with little brown touches, whilst the larger feathers of the wing are black, with each of them a white spot near the middle; those of the neck are whitish with black streaks, and are long and erected when the bird is attacked. The bill is flat like the starling's, nearly an inch and a half long, and the legs agree in shape and in the want of the hinder toe with the bustard's, but it is not, as Golius says, the bustard, that bird being twice as big as the hobara. Nothing can be more entertaining than to see this bird pursued by the hawk, and what a variety of flights and stratagems it makes use of to escape." The French call the hobara, a little bustard, *poule de Carthage,* or Carthage-fowl. They are frequently sold in the market of Tunis, as ordinary fowls, but eat something like pheasant, and their flesh is red.

feathers on its head, and ruffle of long black feathers, which they stretch out at pleasure, with a large grey eye. A curious prickly plant grows about here, something like a dwarf broom, if its leaves were sharp thorns, it is called Kardert. The Bey made R. a present of the hobara.

One day three gazelles were caught, and also a fox, by R.'s greyhound, which behaved extremely well, and left the other dogs in the rear, every now and then attacking him in the hind-quarters. Saw seven or eight hobaras, but too windy for the hawks to be flown. Captain B. chased a gazelle himself, and had the good fortune to catch him. As soon as an Arab secures an animal, he immediately cuts its throat, repeating "Bismillah, Allah Akbar," " In the name (of God), God is great."

We marched seventeen miles to a place called Aly Ben Own, the name of the saint buried close by. The plain we crossed must have been once thickly inhabited, as there were many remains. We were joined by more Arabs, and our force continued to augment. The Bey, being in want of horses, the same system of seizing them was adopted as with the camels.

One splendid morning that broke over our encampment we had an opportunity of witnessing Africa's most gorgeous scenery.* Plenty of hobaras; they fly like a goose. The hawks took two or three of them, also some hares. The poor hare does not know what to make of

---

* The most grandly beautiful view in Tunis is that from the Belvidere, about a mile north-west from the capital, looking immediately over the Marsa road. Here, on a hill of very moderate elevation, you have the most beautiful as well as the most magnificent panoramic view of sea and lake, mountain and plain, town and village, in the whole Regency, or perhaps in any other part of North Africa. There are besides many lovely walks around the capital, particularly among and around the craggy heights of the south-east. But these are little frequented by the European residents, the women especially, who are so stay-at-homeative that the greater part of them never walked round the suburbs once in their lives. Europeans generally prefer the Marina, lined on each side, not with pleasant trees, but dead animals, sending forth a most offensive smell.

the hawks; after a little running, it gives itself up for death, only first dodging out of the bird's pounce, or hiding itself in a tuft of grass or a bush, but which it is not long allowed to do, for the Arabs soon drive it out from its vain retreat. The hawk, when he seizes the hare with one claw, catches hold of any tuft of grass or irregularity of the ground with the other; a strong leather strap is also fastened from one leg to the other, to prevent them from being pulled open or strained. We came upon a herd of small deer, called ebba, which are a little larger than the gazelle, but they soon bounded beyond our pursuit, leaving us scarcely time to admire their delicate make and unapproachable speed.

We crossed a range of hills into another plain, at the extremity of which lies Ghafsa. The surface was naked, with the exception of tufts of strong, rushy grass, almost a sure indication of hares, and of which we started a great number. We saw another description of bird, called rhaad,* with white wings, which flew like a pigeon, but more swiftly. Near our tract were the remains of a large tank of ancient Roman construction. The Bey shot a fox. Marched fourteen or fifteen miles to Zwaneah, which means " little garden," though there is no sign of such thing, unless it be the few oranges, dates, and pomegranates which they find here. We had water from a tank of modern construction; some remains were close to the camp, the ancient cistern and stone duct leading from the hills. We had two thousand camels with the camp and following it, for which

---

* Shaw says: " The rhaad, or safsaf, is a granivorous and gregarious bird, which wanteth the hinder toe. There are two species, and both about and a little larger than the ordinary pullet. The belly of both is white, back and wings of a buff colour spotted with brown, tail lighter and marked all along with black transverse streaks, beak and legs stronger than the partridge. The name rhaad, " thunder," is given to it from the noise it makes on the ground when it rises, safsaf, from its beating the air, a sound imitating the motion."

not a single atom of provender is carried, the camels subsisting scantily upon the coarse grass, weeds or thorns, which the soil barely affords. The camel is very fond of sharp, prickly thorns. You look upon the animal, with its apparently most tender mouth, chopping the sharpest thorns it can find, full of amazement! Some of the chiefs who have lately joined us, have brought their wives with them, riding on camels in a sort of palanquin or shut-up machine. These palanquins have a kind of mast and shrouds, from which a bell is slung, tinkling with the swinging motion of the camel. This rude contrivance makes the camel more than ever "the ship of the Desert." Several fine horses were brought in as presents to the Bey, one a very fine mare.

Our next march was towards Ghafsa, about twenty miles off. We were joined by a considerable number of fresh Arabs, who " played at powder," and kept firing and galloping before the Bey the whole day; some of them managed themselves and their arms and horses with great address, balancing the firelock on their heads, firing it, twisting it round, throwing it into the air, and catching it again, and all without once losing the command of their horses. An accident happened amidst the fun; two of the parties came in contact, and one of them received a dreadful gash on the forehead. The dresses of some of them were very rich, and looked very graceful on horseback. A ride over sand-hills brought us in view of the town, embedded in olive and date-trees, looking fresh and green after our hot and dusty march; it lay stretched at the foot of a range of hills, which formed the boundaries of another extensive plain.

We halted at Ghafsa,* which is almost a

* Ghafsa, whose name Bochart derives from the Hebrew "comprimere," is an ancient city, claiming as its august founder, the Libyan Hercules. It was one of the principal towns in the dominions of Jugurtha, and well-fortified, rendered secure by being placed in the midst of immense deserts, fabled to have been inhabited solely by snakes and serpents.

mass of rubbish filled with dirty people, although there are plenty of springs about, principally hot and mineral waters. Although the Moors, by their religion, are enjoined the constant use of the bath, yet because they do not

Marius took it by a *coup-de-main*, and put all the inhabitants to the sword. The modern city is built on a gentle eminence, between two arid mountains, and, in a great part, with the materials of the ancient one. Ghafsa has no wall of *enceinte*, or rather a ruined wall surrounds it, and is defended by a kasbah, containing a small garrison. This place may be called the gate of the Tunisian Sahara; it is the limit of Blad-el-Jereed; the sands begin now to disappear, and the land becomes better, and more suited to the cultivation of corn. Three villages are situated in the environs, Sala, El-Kesir, and El-Ghetar. A fraction of the tribe of Hammand deposit their grain in Ghafsa. This town is famous for its manufactories of baracans and blankets ornamented with pretty coloured flowers. There is also a nitre and powder-manufactory, the former obtained from the earth by a very rude process.

The environs are beautifully laid out in plantations of the fig, the pomegranate, and the orange, and especially the date-palm, and the olive-tree. The oil made here is of peculiarly good quality, and is exported to Tugurt, and other oases of the Desert.

change their linen and other clothes, they are always very dirty. They do not, however, exceed the Maltese and Sicilians, and many other people of the neighbourhood, in filth, and perhaps the Moors are cleaner in their habits than they. The Arabs are extremely disgusting, and their women are often seen in a cold winter's evening, standing with their legs extended over a smoky wood fire, holding up their petticoats, and continuing in this indelicate position for hours together.

In these Thermæ, or hot, sulphurous, and other mineral springs, is the phenomenon of the existence of fish and small snakes. These were observed by our tourists, but I shall give three other authorities besides them. Shaw says: "'The Ouri-el-Nout,' *i.e.*, 'Well of Fish,' and the springs of Ghasa and Toser, nourish a number of small fishes of the mullet and perch kind, and are of an easy digestion. Of the like quality are the other waters of the Jereed, all of them, after they become cold, being the common drink of the inhabitants." Sir Grenville Temple remarks: "The thermometer in the water marked ninety-five degrees; and, what is curious, a considerable number of fish is found in this stream, which measure from four to six inches in length, and resemble, in some degree, the gudgeon, having a delicate flavour. Bruce mentions a similar fact, but he says he saw it in the springs of Feriana. Part of the ancient structure of these baths still exists, and pieces of inscriptions are observed in different places."

Mr. Honneger has made a sketch of this fish, The wood-cut represents it one half the natural size:

The snake, not noticed by former tourists, has been observed by Mr. Honneger, which nourishes itself entirely upon the fish. The wood-cut represents the snake half its natural size:

The fish and the snake live together, though not very amicably, in the hot-springs. Prince Pükler Muskau, who travelled in Tunis, narrates that, "Near the ruins of Utica was a warm spring, in whose almost hot waters we found several turtles, *which seemed to inhabit this basin.*"

However, perhaps, there is no such extraordinary difficulty in the apprehension of this phenomenon, for " The Gulf Stream," on leaving the Gulf of Mexico, has a temperature of more than 27° (centigrade), or $80\frac{6}{10}$ degrees of Fahrenheit."*

Many a fish must pass through and live in this stream. And after all, since water is the element of fish, and is hotter or colder in all regions, like the air, the element of man, which he breathes, warmer or cooler, according to clime and local cirumstances—there appear to be no physical objections in the way of giving implicit credence to our tourists.

Water is so abundant, that the adjoining plain might be easily irrigated, and planted with ten thousand palms and forests of olives. God is bountiful in the Desert, but man wilfully

---

* Kæmtz's Meteorology, p. 191.

neglects these aqueous riches springing up eternally to repair the ravages of the burning simoum! In one of the groves we met a dervish, who immediately set about charming our Boab. He began by an incantation, then seized him round the middle, and, stooping a little, lifted him on his shoulders, continuing the while the incantation. He then put him on his feet again, and, after several attempts, appeared to succeed in bringing off his stomach something in the shape of leaden bullets, which he then, with an air of holy swagger, presented to the astonished guard of the Bey. The dervish next spat on his patient's hands, closed them in his own, then smoothed him down the back like a mountebank smooths his pony, and stroked also his head and beard; and, after further gentle and comely ceremonies of this sort, the charming of the charmer finished, and the Boab presented the holy man with his fee. We dined at the Kaëd's house; this functionary was a very venerable man, a perfect picture of a patriarch of the olden Scriptural times of Abraham, Isaac, and Jacob. There was not a single article of furniture in the room, except a humble sofa, upon which he sat.

We inspected the old Kasbah at Ghafsa, which is in nearly a state of ruin, and looked as if it would soon be down about our ears. It is an irregular square, and built chiefly of the remains of ancient edifices. It was guarded by fifty Turks, whose broken-down appearance was in perfect harmony with the citadel they inhabited. The square in a building is the favourite form of the Moors and Mohammedans generally; the Kaaba of Mecca, the *sanctum sanctorum,* is a square. The Moors endeavour to imitate the sacred objects of their religion in every way, even in the commonest affairs of human existence, whilst likewise their troops of wives and concubines are only an earthly foretaste and an earnest of the celestial ladies they expect to meet hereafter.

We saw them making oil, which was in a very primitive fashion. The oil-makers were nearly all women. The olives were first ground between stones worked by the hands, until they became of the consistence of paste, which was then taken down to the stream and put into a wooden tub with water. On being stirred up, the oil rises to the top, which they skim off with their hands and put into skins or jars; when thus skimmed, they pass the grounds or refuse through a sieve, the water running off; the stones and pulp are then saved for firing. But in this way much of the oil is lost, as may be seen by the greasy surface of the water below where this rude process is going on. Among the oil-women, we noticed a girl who would have been very pretty and fascinating had she washed herself instead of the olives. We entered an Arab house inhabited by some twenty persons, chiefly women, who forthwith unceremoniously took off our caps, examined very minutely all our clothes with an excited curiosity, laughed heartily when we put our hands in our pockets, and wished to do the same, and then pulled our hair, looking under our faces with amorous glances. On the hill overlooking the town, we also met two women screaming frightfully and tearing their faces; we learned that one of them had lost her child. The women make the best blankets here with hand-looms, and do the principal heavy work.

We saw some hobaras, also a bird called getah, smaller than a partridge, something like a ptarmigan, with its summer feathers, and head shaped like a quail. The Bey sent two live ones to R., besides a couple of large jerboahs of this part, called here, *gundy*. They are much like the guinea-pig, but of a sandy colour, and very soft and fine, like a young hare. The jerboahs in the neighbourhood of Tunis are certainly more like the rat. The other day, near the south-west gates, we fell in with a whole colony of them—which, however, were the lesser animal, or Jerd species—who occupied an entire eminence to themselves, the sovereignty of which seemed to have been conceded to them by the Bey of Tunis. They looked upon us as intruders, and came very near to us, as if asking us why we had the audacity to disturb the tranquillity of their republic. The ground here in many places was covered with a substance like the rime of a frosty morning; it tastes like salt, and from it they get nitre. Captain B. thinks it was salt. The water which we drank was brought from Ghafsa: the Bey drinks water brought from Tunis. We marched across a vast plain, covered with the salt just mentioned, which was congealed in shining heaps around bushes or tufts of grass, and among which also scampered a few hares. We encamped at a place called Ghorbatah. Close to the camp was a small shallow stream, on each side of which grew many canes; we bathed in the stream, and felt much refreshed. The evening was pleasantly cool, like a summer evening in England, and reminded us of the dear land of our birth. Numerous plains in North Africa are covered with saline and nitrous efflorescence; to the presence of these minerals is owing the inexhaustible fertility of the soil, which hardly ever receives any manure, only a little stubble being occasionally burnt.

We saw flights of the getah, and of another bird called the gedur, nearly the same, but rather lighter in colour. When they rise from the ground, they make a curious noise, something like a partridge. We were unusually surprised by a flight of locusts, not unlike grasshoppers, of about two inches long, and of a reddish colour. Saw also gazelles. Halted by the dry bed of a river, called Furfouwy. A pool supplied the camp: in the mountains, at a distance, there was, however, a delicious spring, a stream of liquid pearls in these thirsty lands! A bird called mokha appeared now and then; it is about the size of a nightingale, and of a white light-brown colour. We seldom heard such sweet notes as this bird possesses.

Its flying is beautifully novel and curious; it runs on the ground, and now and then stops and rises about fifteen feet from the surface, giving, as it ascends, two or three short slow whistles, when it opens its graceful tail and darts down to the ground, uttering another series of melodious whistles, but much quicker than when it rises.

We continued our march over nearly the same sort of country, but all was now flat as far as the eye could see, the hills being left behind us. About eight miles from Furfouwy, we came to a large patch of date-trees, watered by many springs, but all of them hot. Under the grateful shade of the lofty palm were flowers and fruits in commingled sweetness and beauty. Here was the village of Dra-el-Hammah, surrounded, like all the towns of the Jereed, with date-groves and gardens. The houses were most humbly built of mud and bricks. After a scorching march, we encamped just beyond, having made only ten miles. Saw quantities of bright soft spar, called talc. Here also the ground was covered with a saline effloresence. Near us were put up about a dozen blue cranes, the only birds seen to-day. A gazelle was caught, and others chased. We particularly observed huge patches of ground covered with salt, which, at a distance, appeared just like water.

## CHAPTER X.

Toser.—The Bey's Palace.—Blue Doves.—The town described.—Industry of the People.—Sheikh Tahid imprisoned and punished.—Leghma.—The Boo-habeeba.—A Domestic Picture.—The Bey's Diversions.—The Bastinado.—Concealed Treasure.—Nefta.—The Two Saints.—Departure of Santa Maria.—Snake-charmers.—Wedyen.—Deer-Stalking. —Splendid view of the Sahara.—Revolting Acts.—Ghortabah.—Ghafsa.—Byrlafee.—Mortality among the Camels —Aqueduct.—Remains of Udina.—Arrival at Tunis.—The Boab's Wives.—Curiosities.—Tribute Collected.—Author takes leave of the Governor of Mogador, and embarks for England.—Rough Weather.—Arrival in London.

LEAVING Dra-el-Hammah, after a hot march of five or six miles, we arrived at the top of a rising ground, at the base of which was situate the famous Toser, the head-quarters of the camp in the Jereed, and as far as it goes. Behind the city was a forest of date-trees, and beyond these and all around, as far as the eye could wander, was an immeasurable waste—an ocean of sand—a great part of which we could have sworn was water, unless told to the contrary. We were met, before entering Toser, with some five or six hundred Arabs, who galloped before the Bey, and fired as usual. The people stared at us Christians with open mouths; our dress apparently astonished them. At Toser, the Bey left his tent and entered his palace, so called in courtesy to his Highness, but a large barn of a house, without any pretensions. We had also a room allotted to us in this palace, which was the best to be found in the town, though a small dark affair. Toser is a miserable assemblage of mud and brick huts, of very small dimensions, the beams and the doors being all of date-wood. The gardens, however, under the date-trees are beautiful, and abundantly watered with copious streams, all of which are warm, and in one of which we bathed ourselves and felt new vigour run through our veins. We took a walk in the gardens, and were surprised at the quantities of doves fluttering among the date-trees; they were the common blue or Barbary doves. In the environs of Mogador, these doves are the principal birds shot.

Toser, or Touzer, the *Tisurus* of ancient geography, is a considerable town of about six thousand souls, with several villages in its neighbourhood.

The impression of Toser made upon our tourists agrees with that of the traveller, Desfontaines, who writes of it in 1784:—" The Bey pitched his tent on the right side of the city, if such can be called *a mass of mud-houses.*" The description corresponds also with that of Dr. Shaw, who says that " the villages of the Jereed are built of mud-walls and rafters of palm-trees." Evidently, however, some improvement has been made of late years. The Arabs of Toser, on the contrary, and which was very natural, protested to the French scientific commission that Toser was the finest city in El-Jereed. They pretend that it has an area as large as Algiers, surrounded with a mud wall, twelve or fifteen feet high, and crenated. In the centre is a vast open space, which serves for a market-place. Toser has mosques, schools, Moorish baths—a luxury rare on the confines of the Desert, fondouks or inns, &c. The houses have flat terraces, and are generally well-constructed, the greater part built from the ruins of a Roman town; but many are now dilapidated from the common superstitious cause of not repairing or rebuilding old houses. The choice material for building is brick, mostly unbaked or sun-dried.

Most of these houses stand detached.

Toser, situate in a plain, is commanded from the north-west by a little rocky mountain, whence an abundant spring takes its source, called *Meshra*, running along the walls of the city southward, divides itself afterwards in three branches, waters the gardens, and, after having irrigated the plantations of several other villages, loses itself in the sand at a short distance. The wells within the city of Toser are insufficient for the consumption of the inhabitants, who fetch water from Wad Meshra. The neighbouring villages are Belad-el-Ader, Zin, Abbus; and the sacred villages are Zaouweeat, of Tounseea, Sidi Ali Bou Lifu, and Taliraouee. The Arabs of the open country, and who deposit their grain in and trade with these villages, are Oulad Sidi Sheikh, Oulad Sidi Abeed, and Hammania. The dates of Toser are esteemed of the finest quality.

Walked about the town; several of the inhabitants are very wealthy. The dead saints are, however, here, and perhaps everywhere else in Tunis, more decently lodged, and their marabets are real "whitewashed sepulchres." They make many burnouses at Toser, and every house presents the industrious sight of the needle or shuttle quickly moving. We tasted the leghma, or "tears of the date," for the first time, and rather liked it. On going to shoot doves, we, to our astonishment, put up a snipe.

The weather was very hot; went to shoot doves in the cool of the evening. The Bey administers justice, morning and evening, whilst in the Jereed. An Arab made a present of a fine young ostrich to the Bey, which his Highness, after his arrival in Tunis, sent to R. The great man here is the Sheikh Tahid, who was imprisoned for not having the tribute ready for the Bey. The tax imposed is equivalent to two bunches for each date-tree. The Sheikh has to collect them, paying a certain yearly sum when the Bey arrives, a species of farming-out. It was said that he is very rich, and could well find the money. The dates are almost the only food here, and the streets are literally gravelled with their stones. Santa Maria again returned his horse to the Bey, and got another in its stead. He is certainly a man of *delicate* feeling. This gentleman carried his impudence so far that he even threatened some of the Bey's officers with the supreme wrath of the French Government, unless they attended better to his orders. A new Sheikh was installed, a good thing for the Bey's officers, as many of them got presents on the occasion.

We blessed our stars that a roof was over our heads to shield us from the burning sun. We blew an ostrich-egg, had the contents cooked, and found it very good eating. They are sold for fourpence each, and it is pretended that one makes an ample meal for twelve persons. We are supplied with leghma every morning; it tastes not unlike cocoa-nut milk, but with more body and flavour. R. very unwell, attributed it to his taking copious draughts of the leghma. Rode out of an evening; there was a large encampment of Arabs outside the town, thoroughly sun-burnt, hardy-looking fellows, some of them as black as negroes. Many people in Toser have sore eyes, and several with the loss of one eye, or nearly so; opthalmia, indeed, is the most prevalent disease in all

Barbary. The neighbourhood of the Desert, where the greater part of the year the air is filled with hot particles of sand, is very unfavourable to the sight; the dazzling whiteness of the whitewashed houses also greatly injures the eyes. But the Moors pretend that lime-washing is necessary to the preservation of the houses from the weather, as well as from filth of all sorts. We think really it is useful, by preventing dirty people in many cases from being eaten up by their own filth and vermin, particularly the Jews, the Tunisian Jews being the dirtiest persons in the Regency. The lime-wash is the grand *sanitary* instrument in North Africa.

There are little birds that frequent the houses, that might be called Jereed sparrows, and which the Arabs name boo-habeeba, or "friend of my father;" but their dress and language are very different, having reddish breasts, being of a small size, and singing prettily. Shaw mentions them under the name of the Capsa-sparrow, but he is quite wrong in making them as large as the common house-sparrow. He adds: "It is all over of a lark-colour, excepting the breast, which is somewhat lighter, and shineth like that of a pigeon. The boo-habeeba has a note infinitely preferable to that of the canary, or nightingale." He says that all attempts to preserve them alive out of the districts of the Jereed have failed. R. has brought several home from that country, which were alive whilst I was in Tunis. There are also many at the Bardo in cages, that live in this way as long as other birds.

Went to see the houses of the inhabitants: they were nearly all the same, the furniture consisting of a burnouse-loom, a couple of millstones, and a quantity of basins, plates, and dishes, hung upon the walls for effect, seldom being used; there were also some skins of grain. The beams across the rooms, which are very high, are hung with onions, dates, and pomegranates; the houses are nearly all of one story. Some of the women are pretty, with large long black eyes and lashes; they colour the lower lid black, which does not add to their beauty, though it shows the bewitching orb more fully and boldly. They were exceedingly dirty and ragged, wearing, nevertheless, a profusion of ear-rings, armlets, anclets, bracelets, and all sorts of *lets*, with a thousand talismanic charms hanging from their necks upon their ample bosoms, which latter, from the habit of not wearing stays, reach as low down as their waists. They wrap up the children in swaddling-clothes, and carry them behind their backs when they go out.

Two men were bastinadoed for stealing a horse, and not telling where they put him; every morning they were to be flogged until they divulged their hiding-place.

A man brought in about a foot of horse's skin, on which was the Bey's mark, for which he received another horse. This is always done when any animal dies belonging to the Beys, the man in whose hands the animal is, receiving a new one on producing the part of the skin marked. The Bey and his ministers and mamelukes amused themselves with shooting at a mark. The Bey made some good hits.

The Bey and his mamelukes also took diversion in spoiling the appearance of a very nice young horse; they daubed hieroglyphics upon his shoulders and loins, and dyed the back where the saddle is placed, and the three legs below the knee with henna, making the other leg look as white as possible. Another grey horse, a very fine one, was also cribbed. We may remark here, that there were very few fine horses to be met with, all the animals looking poor and miserable, whilst these few fine ones fell into the hands of the Bey. It is probable, however, that the Arabs kept their best and most beautiful horses out of the way, while the camp was moving among them.

The old Sheikh still continued in prison. The bastinadoes with which he had been treated were inflicted on his bare person, cold water being applied thereto, which made the punishment more severe. After receiving one hundred, he said he would shew his hiding-place; and some people being sent with him, dug a hole where he pointed out, but without coming to anything. This was done several times, but with the same effect. He was then locked up in chains till the following morning. Millions of dollars lie buried by the Arabs at this moment in different parts of Barbary, especially in Morocco, perhaps the half of which will never be found, the owners of them having died before they could point out their hoarded treasures to their relatives, as but a single person is usually in the secret. Money is in this way buried by tribes, who have nothing whatever to fear from their sovereigns and their sheikhs; they do it from immemorial custom. It is for this reason the Arabs consider that under all ancient ruins heaps of money are buried, placed there by men or demons, who hold the shining hoards under their invincible spell. They cannot comprehend how European tourists can undertake such long journeys, merely for the purpose of examining old heaps of stones, and making plans and pictures of such rubbish. When any person attempts to convince the Arabs that this is the sole object, they only laugh with incredulity.

Went to Nefta, a ride of about fourteen miles, lying somewhat nearer the Sahara than Toser. The country on the right was undulating sand, on the left an apparently boundless ocean, where lies, as a vast sheet of liquid fire, when the sun shines on it, the now long celebrated Palus Libya. In this so-called lake no water is visible, except a small marsh like the one near Toser, where we went duck-shooting. Our party was very respectable, consisting of the Agha of the Arabs, two or three of the Bey's mamelukes, the Kaëd of the Jereed, whose name is Braun, and fifty or sixty Arab guards, besides ourselves. On entering Nefta, the escort immediately entered, according to custom, a marabet (that of Sidi Bou Aly), Captain B. and R. meanwhile standing outside.

There were two famous saints here, one of whom was a hundred years of age. The other, Sidi Mustapha Azouz, had the character of being a very clever and good man, which also his intelligent and benevolent appearance betokened, and not a fanatic, like Amour Abeda of Kairwan. There were at the time of our visit to him about two hundred people in his courtyard, who all subsisted on his charities. We were offered dates, kouskousou,* and a seed which they call sgougou, and which has the appearance of dried apple-seed. The Arabs eat it with honey, first dipping their fingers into the honey, and then into the seed, which deliciously sticks to the honey. The Sheikh's saint also distributed beads and rosaries. He gave R. a bag of sgougou-seed, as well as some beads. These two Sheikhs are objects of most religious veneration

* This is the national dish of Barbary, and is a preparation of wheat-flour granulated, boiled by the steam of meat. It is most nutritive, and is eaten with or without meat and vegetables. When the grains are large, it is called hamza.

amongst all true believers, and there is nothing which would not be done at their bidding.

Nefta, the Negeta of the ancients, is the frontier town of the Tunisian territories from the south, being five days' journey, or about thirty-five or forty leagues from the oases of Souf, and fifteen days' from Ghadumes. Nefta is not so much a town as an agglomeration of villages, separated from one another by gardens, and occupying an extent of surface twice the size that of the city of Algiers. These villages are Hal Guema, Mesâba, Zebda Ouled, Sherif, Beni Zeid, Beni Ali, Sherfa, and Zaouweeah Sidi Ahmed.

The position of Nefta and its environs is very picturesque. Water is here abundant. The principal source, which, under the name of Wad Nefta, takes its rise at the north of the city, in the midst of a movement of earth, enters the villages of Sherfa and Sidi Ahmed; divides them in two, and fecundates its gardens planted with orange-trees, pomegranates, and fig-trees.

The same spring, by the means of ducts of earth, waters a forest of date-trees which extends some leagues. A regulator of the water (kaëd-el-ma) distributes it to each proprietor of the plantation.

The houses of Nefta are built generally of brick; some with taste and luxury; the interior is ornamented with Dutch tiles brought from Tunis. Each quarter has its mosque and school, and in the centre of the group of villages is a place called Rebot, on the banks of Wad Nefta, which serves for a common market. Here are quarters specially devoted to the aristocratic landed proprietors, and others to the busy merchants. The Shereefs are the genuine nobles, or seigneurs of Nefta, from among whom the Bey is wont to choose the Governors of the city. The complexion of the population is dark, from its alliance with Negress slaves, like most towns advanced in the Desert. The manners of the people are pure. They are strict observers of the law, and very hospitable to strangers. Captain B., however, thought that, had he not been under the protection of the Bey, his head would not have been worth much in these districts. Every traveller almost forms a different opinion, and frequently the very opposite estimate, respecting the strangers amongst whom he is sojourning. A few Jewish artizans have always been tolerated here, on condition of wearing a black handkerchief round their heads, and not mount a horse, &c. Recently the Bey, however, by solemn decrees, has placed the Jews exactly on the same footing of rights and privileges as the rest of his subjects.

Nefta is the intermediate *entrepôt* of commerce which Tunis pours towards the Sahara, and for this reason is called by the Arabs, "the gate of Tunis;" but the restrictive system established by the Turks during late years at Ghadumes, has greatly damaged the trade between the Jereed and the Desert. The movement of the markets and caravans takes place at the beginning of spring, and at the end of summer. Only a portion of the inhabitants is devoted to commerce, the rich landed proprietory and the Shereefs representing the aristocracy, lead the tranquil life of nobles, the most void of care, and, perhaps, the happiest of which contemplative philosophy ever dreamed. The oasis of Nefta, indeed, is said to be the most poetic of the Desert; its gardens are delicious; its oranges and lemons sweet; its dates the finest fruit in the "land of dates." Nearly all the women are pretty, of that beauty peculiar to the Oriental race; and the ladies who do not expose themselves to the fierce sun of the day, are as fair as Mooresses.

Santa Maria left for Ghabs, to which place there is not a correct route laid down in any chart. There are three routes, but the wells of one are only known to travellers, a knowledge which cannot be dispened with in these dry regions. The wells of the other two routes are known to the bordering tribes alone, who, when they have taken a supply of water, cover them up with sand, previously laying a camel-skin over the well-mouth, to prevent the sand falling into the water, so that, while dying with thirst, you might be standing on a well and be none the wiser. The Frenchman has taken with him an escort of twelve men. The weather is cooler, with a great deal of wind, raising and darkening the sky with sand; even among the date-groves our eyes and noses were like so many sand-quarries.

Sheikh Tahib has been twice subjected to corporal punishment in the same way as before mentioned, with the addition of fifty, but they cannot make him bleed as they wish. He declares he has not got the money, and that he cannot pay them, though they cut him to pieces. As he has collected a great portion of the tribute of the people, one cannot much pity the lying rogue.

We were amused with the snake-charmers. These gentry are a company under the protection of their great saint Sidi Aysa, who has long gone upwards, but also is now profitably employed in helping the juggling of these snake-mountebanks. These fellows take their snakes about in small bags or boxes, which are perfectly harmless, their teeth and poison-bags being extracted. They carry them in their bosoms, put them in their mouths, stuffing a long one in of some feet in length, twist them around their arms, use them as a whip to frighten the people, in the meanwhile screaming out and crying unto their Heavenly protector for help, the bystanders devoutly joining in their prayers. The snake-charmers usually perform other tricks, such as swallowing nails and sticking an iron bar in their eyes; and they wear their hair long like women, which gives them a very wild maniacal look.

Three of the mamelukes and ourselves went to Wedyen, a town and date-wood about eight miles from Toser, to the left. The date-grove is extensive, and there are seven villages in it of the same name. We slept in the house of the Sheikh, who complained that the Frenchman, in passing that way, had allowed his escort to plunder, and actually bound the poor Sheikh, threatening him on his remonstrating. What conduct for Christians to teach these people!

One morning before daylight, we were on horseback, and *en route* towards the hills, for the purpose of shooting loted, as they call a species of deer found here. The ground in the neighbourhood of Wedyen is tossed about like a hay-field, and volcanic looking. About four miles off we struck into the rocks, on each side of our path, rising perpendicularly in fantastic shapes. On reaching the highest ground, the view was exceedingly wild. Much of the rock appeared as if it had only just been cooled from a state of fusion; there was also a quantity of tuffo rock, similar to that in the neighbourhood of Naples. The first animal we saw was a wolf, which, standing on the sky-line of the opposite hill, looked gigantic. The deep valley between, however, prevented our nearer approach.

We soon after came on a loted, who took to his heels, turning round a mass of rock; but, soon after, he almost met us, and we had a view of him within forty yards. Several shots were fired at him without effect, and he at last made his escape, with a speed which defied all our attempts at following him. Dismounting, the Sheikh Ali, of the Arab tribe Hammama, who was with us, and who is the greatest deer-stalker in the country, preceded us a little distance to look out for deer, the marks of which were here very numerous. After a short time, an Arab brought information of a herd of some thirty, with a good many young ones; but our endeavours to have a shot at them were fruitless, though one of the Arabs got near enough to loose the dogs at them, and a greyhound was kicked over for his pains. We saw no more of them; but our want of success was not surprising, silence not being in the least attended to, and our party was far too large. The Arabs have such a horrible habit of vociferation, that it is a wonder they ever take any game at all. About the hills was scattered a great variety of aromatic plants, quantities of shells, and whole oyster-beds, looking almost as fresh as if they had been found by the sea-side.

On our return from Toser, we had an extensive view of the Sahara, an ocean as far as the eye could see, of what one would have taken his oath was water, the shores, inlets, and bays being clearly defined, but, in reality, nothing but salt scattered on the surface. Several islets were apparently breaking its watery expanse, but these also were only heaps of sand raised from the surrounding flat. The whole country, hills, plains and deserts, gave us an idea as if the materials had been thrown together for manufacture, and had never been completed. Nevertheless these savage deserts of boundless extent are as complete in their kind as the smiling meadows and fertile corn-fields of England, each being perfect in itself, necessary to the grand whole of creation, and forming an essential portion of the works of Divine Providence.

The Sheikh Tahib's gardens were sold for 15,000 piastres, his wife also added to this 1,000, and he was set at liberty. The dates have been coming in to a great amount. There are many different kinds. The principal are:—Degalah, the most esteemed, which are very sweet and almost transparent. Captain B. preferred the Trungah, another first-rate sort, which are plum-shaped, and taste something like a plum. There are also the Monachah, which are larger than the other two, dryer and more mealy, and not so sweet as Degalah, and other sorts. The dates were very fine, though in no very great abundance, the superior state of ripeness being attributed to there only being a single day of rain during the past year in the Jereed. Rain is bad for the dates, but the roots of the tree cannot have too much water.

The tent-pitchers of the camp went round and performed, in mask, actions of the most revolting description, some being dressed as women, and dancing in the most lascivious and indecent manner. One fellow went up to R., who was just on the point of knocking him down, when, seeing the Treasurer of the Bey cracking his sides with laughter, he allowed the brute to go off under such high patronage. It was even said that these fellows were patronized by his Highness. But, on all Moorish feast-days, lascivious actions of men and women are an indispensable part of their entertainment. This is the worst side of the character of the Moors. The Moorish women were never so profligate as since the arrival of the French in Algeria.

One of the greatest chiefs, Sultan Kaëd, of the Hammama has just died. He was an extremely old man, and it is certain that people live to a good old age in this burning clime. During his life, he had often distinguished himself, and lastly against the French, before Constantina. Whilst in the hills one day, we came suddenly upon a set of Arabs, about nine in number, who took to their heels on seeing us. A man has just been killed near this place, probably by the same gang. For robbery and murder, no hills could be better fitted, the passes being so intricate, and the winds and turns so sudden and sharp. The Sheikh Ali brought in two loteds, a female and its young one, which he had shot. The head of the loted is like a deer's, but the eye is further up: it is about a fallow-deer's size. The female has not the beard like a goat, but long hair, reaching from the head to the bottom of the chest, and over the fore-legs. These loteds were taken in consequence of an order from the Bey, that they should not return without some.

On our march back to Tunis, we encamped for two days by the foot of a range of hills at Sheesheeah, about ten miles off. The water, brought from some distance, was bad and salt.

We proceeded to Ghortabah, our old place. Two of the prisoners (about twelve of whom we had with us), and one of the Turks, died from the excessive heat. The two couriers that were sent with despatches for the Government were attacked near this place by the Arabs, and the horse of one was so injured, that it was necessary to kill him; the man who rode the horse was also shot through the leg. This was probably in revenge for the exactions of the Bey of the Camp on the tribes.

On our return to Ghafsa, we had rain, hail, and high wind, and exceedingly cold—a Siberian winter's day on the verge of the scorching desert. The ground, where there was clay, very slippery; the camels reeled about as if intoxicated. The consequence was, it was long before the tents came up, and we endured much from this sudden change of the weather. Our sufferings were, however, nothing as compared to others, for during the day, ten men were brought in dead, from the cold (three died four days before from heat), principally Turks; and, had there been no change in the temperature, we cannot tell how many would have shared the same fate. Many of the camels, struggling against the clayey soil, could not come up.

Eight more men were shortly buried, and three were missing. The sudden transition from the intense heat of the one day to the freezing cold of the next, probably gave the latter a treble power, producing these disastrous effects, the poor people being sadly ill-clad, and quite unprepared for such extreme rigour. Besides, on our arrival at the camp, all the money in Europe could not have purchased us the required comforts, or rather necessaries, to preserve our health. Cold makes everybody very selfish. We were exceedingly touched on hearing of the death of a little girl, whom we saw driven out of a kitchen, in which the poor helpless little thing had taken refuge from the inclemency of the weather.

Santa Maria arrived from Ghabs without accident, having scarcely seen a soul the whole of the way. He certainly was an enterprizing fellow, worthy of imitation. He calculated the distance from Ghabs to Toser at 200 miles. There are a number of towns in the districts of Ghabs better built than those of Nefta and Toser; Ghabs river is also full of water and the soil of the country is very fertile. The dates are not so good as those of the Jereed. Ghabs is about 130 miles from Ghafsa. We here took our farewell of Santa Maria; he went to Beja, the head-quarters of the summer-camp: thence, of course, he would proceed to Algiers, to give an account of his *espionage*. Next season, he said, he would go to Tripoli and Ghadames; he had been many years in North Africa, and spoke Arabic fluently.

We next marched to Byrlafee, about twenty miles, and ninety-one from Toser, where there are the ruins of an old town. The weather continued cold and most wintry. Here is a very ancient well still in use. Fragments of cornices and pillars are strewn about. The foundations of houses, and some massive stone towers, which from their having a pipe up the centre, must have had something to do with regulating the water, are all that remain.

We had now much wind, but no rain. A great many camels and horses perished. Altogether, the number of camels that died on the return of the camp, was 550. The price of a camel varies from 60 to 200 piastres. Many good ones were sold at the camp for eighty piastres each, or about two pounds ten shillings, English money. A good sheep was disposed of for four or five piastres, or about three shillings. There were also some ludicrous sales. A horse in the extremities of nature, or near to the *articulo mortis,* was sold for a piastre, eight pence; a camel, in a like situation, was sold for a piastre and a half. A tolerably good horse in Tunis sells at from 800 to 1000 piastres.

There are the remains of an aqueduct at Gilma, and several other buildings, the capitals of the pillars being elaborately worked. It is seen that nearly the entire surface of Tunis is covered with remains of aqueducts, Roman, Christian, and Moorish. If railways be applied to this country—the French are already talking about forming one from Algiers to Blidah, across the Mitidjah—unquestionably along the lines will be constructed ducts for water, which could thus be distributed over the whole country. Instead of the camels of the " Bey of the Camp" carrying water from Tunis to the Jereed, the railway would take from Zazwan, the best and most delicious water in the Regency, to the dry deserts of the Jereed, with the greatest facility. As to railways paying in this country, the resources of Tunis, if developed, could pay anything.

Marching onwards about eighteen miles, we

encamped two or three beyond an old place called Sidi-Ben-Habeeba. A man murdered a woman from jealousy in the camp, but made his escape. Almost every eminence we passed was occupied with the remains of some ancient fort, or temple. There was a good deal of corn in small detached patches, but it must be remembered, the north-western provinces are the corn-districts.

In the course of the following three days, we reached Sidi-Mahammedeah, where are the magnificent remains of Udina. After about an hour's halt, and when all the tents had been comfortably pitched, the Bey astonished us with an order to continue our march, and we pursued our way to Momakeeah, about thirty miles, which we did not reach until after dark. We passed, for some three or four hours, through a flight of locusts, the air being darkened, and the ground loaded with them. At a little distance, a flight of locusts has the appearance of a heavy snow-storm. These insects rarely visit the capital; but, since the appearance of those near Momakeeah, they have been collected in the neighbourhood of the city, cooked, and sold among the people. Momakeeah is a country-house belonging to the Bey, to whom, also, belongs a great portion of the land around. There is a large garden, laid out in the Italian style attached to this country-seat.

On arriving at Tunis, we called at the Bardo as we passed, and saw the guard mounting. There was rather a fine band of military music; Moorish musicians, but playing, after the European style, Italian and Moorish airs.

We must give here some account of our Boab's domestic concerns. He boasted that he had had twenty-seven wives, his religion allowing four at once, which he had had several times; he was himself of somewhat advanced years. According to him, if a man quarrels with his wife, he can put her in prison, but must, at the same time, support her. A certain quantity of provision is laid down by law, and he must give her two suits, or changes, of clothes a year. But he must also visit her once a week, and the day fixed is Friday. If the wife wishes to be separated, and to return to her parents, she must first pay the money which he may demand, and must also have his permission, although he himself may send her to her parents whenever he chooses, without assigning any reason. He retains the children, and he may marry again. The woman is generally expected to bring her husband a considerable sum in the way of dowry, but, on separation, she gets nothing back. This was the Boab's account, but I think he has overdone the harshness and injustice of the Mohammedan law of marriage in relating it to our tourists. It may be observed that the strict law is rarely acted upon, and many respectable Moors have told me that they have but one wife, and find that quite enough. It is true that many Moors, especially learned men, divorce their wives when they get old, feeling the women an embarrassment to them, and no wonder, when we consider these poor creatures have no education, and, in their old age, neither afford connubial pleasure nor society to their husbands. With respect to divorce, a woman can demand by law and right to be separated from her husband, or divorced, whenever he ill-treats her, or estranges himself from her. Eunuchs, who have the charge of the women, are allowed to marry, although they cannot have any family. The chief eunuch of the Bardo has the most revolting countenance.

Our tourists brought home a variety of curious Jereed things: small date-baskets full of dates, woollen articles, skins of all sorts, and a few live animals. Sidi Mohammed also made them many handsome presents. Some deer, Jereed goats, an ostrich, &c., were sent to Mr. R. after his return, and both Captain B. and Mr. R. have had every reason to be extremely gratified with the hospitality and kind attentions of the "Bey of the Camp."

It is very difficult to ascertain the amount of tribute collected in the Jereed, some of which, however, was not got in, owing to various impediments. Our tourists say generally :—

|  | Camel-loads.* |
|---|---|
| Money, dollars, and piastres, (chiefly I imagine, the latter.) | 23 |
| Burnouses, blankets, and quilts, &c. | 6 |
| Dates (these were collected at Toser, and brought from Nefta and the surrounding districts) | 500 |
| Total | 529 |

It is impossible, with this statement before us, to make out any exact calculation of the amount of tribute. A cantar of dates varies from fifteen

* A camel-load is about five cantars, and a cantar is a hundred weight.

to twenty-five shillings, say on an average a pound sterling; this will make the amount of the 500 camel-loads at five cantars per load    £2,500

Six camel-loads of woollen manufactures, &c., at sixty pound per load, value    360

Total    . £2,860

The money, chiefly piastres, must be left to conjecture. However, Mr. Levy, a large merchant at Tunis, thinks the amount might be from 150 to 200,000 piastres, or, taking the largest sum, £6,250 sterling:

Total amount of the tribute of the Jereed:
in goods    . £2,860
Ditto, in money:    . 6,250

Total    . £9,110

To this sum may be added the smaller

presents of horses, camels, and other beasts of burden.

\* \* \* \*

Before leaving Mogador, in company with Mr. Willshire, I saw his Excellency, the Governor again, when I took formal leave of him. He accompanied me down to the port with several of the authorities, waiting until I embarked for the Renshaw schooner. Several of the Consuls, and nearly all the Europeans, were also present. On the whole, I was satisfied with the civilities of the Moorish authorities, and offer my cordial thanks to the Europeans of Mogador for their attentions during my residence in that city.

A little circumstance shews the subjection of our merchants, the Consul not excepted, to the Moorish Government. One of the merchants wished to accompany me on board, but was not permitted, on account of his engagements with the Sultan.

A merchant cannot even go off the harbour to superintend the stowing of his goods. Never were prisoners of war, or political offenders, so closely watched as the boasted imperial merchants of this city.

After setting sail, we were soon out of sight of Mogador; and, on the following day, land disappeared altogether. During the next month, we were at sea, and out of view of the shore. I find an entry in my journal, when off the Isle of Wight. We had had most tremendous weather, successive gales of foul wind, from north and north-east. Our schooner was a beautiful vessel, a fine sailer with a flat bottom, drawing little water, made purposely for Barbary ports. She had her bows completely under water, and pitched her way for twenty-five succeeding days, through huge rising waves of sea and foam. During the whole of this time, I never got up, and lived on bread and water with a little biscuit. Captain Taylor, who was a capital seaman, and took the most accurate observations, lost all patience, and, though a good methodist, would now and then rush on deck, and swear at the perverse gale and wrathful sea. We took on board a fine barb for Mr. Elton, which died after a few days at sea, in these tempests. I had a young vulture that died a day before the horse, or we should have fed him on the carcase.

An aoudad which we conveyed on account of Mr. Willshire to London, for the Zoological

Society, outlived these violent gales, and was safely and comfortably lodged in the Regent's Park. After my return from Africa, I paid my brave and hardy fellow-passenger a visit, and find the air of smoky London agrees with him as well as the cloudless region of the Morocco Desert.

# APPENDIX.

# APPENDIX.

The following account of the bombardment of Mogador by the French, written at the period by an English Resident may be of interest at the present time.

Mogador was bombarded on the 13th of August, 1844. Hostilities began at 9 o'clock A.M., by the Moors firing twenty-one guns before the French had taken up their position, but the fire was not returned until 2 P.M. The 'Gemappes,' 100; 'Suffren,' 99; 'Triton,' 80; ships of the line. 'Belle Poule,' 60, frigate; 'Asmodée' and 'Pluton,' steamers, and some brigs, constituted the bombarding squadron. The batteries were silenced, and the Moorish authorities with many of the inhabitants fled, leaving the city unprotected against the wild tribes, who this evening and the next morning, sacked and fired the city. On the 16th, nine hundred French were landed on the isle of Mogador. After a rude encounter with the garrison, they took possession of it and its forts. Their loss was, after twenty-eight hours' bombarding, trifling, some twenty killed and as many more wounded; the Moors lost some five hundred on the isle killed, besides the casualties in the city.

The British Consul and his wife, and Mr. and Mrs. Robertson, with others, were obliged to remain in the town during the bombardment on account of their liabilities to the Emperor. The escape of these people from destruction was most miraculous.

The bombarding squadron reached on the 10th, the English frigate, 'Warspite,' on the 13th, and the wind blowing strong from N.E., and preventing the commencement of hostilities, afforded opportunity to save, if possible, the British Consul's family and other detained Europeans; but, notwithstanding the strenuous remonstrances of the captain of the 'Warspite,' nothing whatever could prevail upon the Moorish Deputy-Governor in command, Sidi Abdallah Deleero, to allow the British and other Europeans to take their departure. The Governor even peremptorily refused permission for the wife of the Consul to leave, upon the cruel sophism that, " The Christian religion asserts the husband and wife to be one, consequently," added the Governor, " as it is my duty, which I owe to my Emperor, to prevent the Consul from leaving Mogador, I must also keep his wife."

The fact is the Moors, in their stupidity, and perhaps in their revenge, thought the retaining of the British Consul and the Europeans might, in some way or other, contribute to the defence of themselves, save the city, or mitigate the havoc of the bombardment. At any rate, they would say, "Let the Christians share the same fate and dangers as ourselves." During the bombardment, the Moors for two hours fought well, but their best gunner, a Spanish renegade, Omar Ei-Haj, being killed, they became dispirited and abandoned the batteries. The Governor and his troops, about sunset, disgracefully and precipitately fled, followed by nearly all the Moorish population, thereby abandoning Mogador to pillage, and the European Jews to the merciless wild tribes, who, though levied to defend the town, had, for some hours past, hovered round it like droves of famished wolves.

As the Governor fled out, terrified as much at the wild tribes as of the French, in rushed these hordes, led on by their desperate chiefs. These wretches undismayed, unmoved by the terrors of the bombarding ravages around, strove and vied with each other in the committal of every act of the most unlicensed ferocity and depredation, breaking open houses, assaulting the inmates, murdering such as shewed resistance, denuding the more submissive of their clothing, abusing women—particularly in the Jewish quarter—to all which atrocities the Europeans were likewise exposed.

At the most imminent hazard of their lives, the British Consul and his wife, with a few others, escaped from these ruffians. Truly providential was their flight through streets, resounding with the most turbulent confusion and sanguinary violence. It was late when the plunderers appeared before the Consulates, where, without any ceremony, by hundreds, they fell to work, breaking open bales of goods, ransacking places for money and other treasures; and, thus unsatisfied in their rapacity, they tore and burnt all the account-books and Consular documents.

Other gangs fought over the spoil; some carrying off their booty, and others setting it on fire. It was a real pandemonium of discord and licentiousness. During the darkness, and in the midst of such scenes, it was that the

Consul and his wife threaded their precarious flight through the streets, and in their way were intercepted by a marauding band, who attacked them; tore off his coat; and, seizing his wife, insisted upon denuding her, four or five daggers being raised to her throat, expecting to fiud money concealed about their persons; nor would the ruffians desist until they ascertained they had none, the Consul having prudently resolved to take no money with them. Fortunately, at this juncture, his wife was able to speak, and in Arabic (being born here, and daughter of a former Consul), therefore she could give force to her entreaties by appealing to them not to imbue their hands in the blood of their countrywomen. This had the desired effect. The chief of the party undertook to conduct them to the water-port, when, coming in contact with another party, a conflict about booty ensued, during which the Consul's family got out of the town to a place of comparative security.

Incidents of a similar alarming nature attended the escape of Mr. Robertson, his wife, and four children; one a baby in arms. In the crowd, Mr. Robertson, with a child in each hand, lost sight of Mrs. Robertson, with her infant and another child. Distracted by sad forebodings, poor Mr. Robertson forced his way to the water-port, but not before a savage mountainer—riding furiously by him—aimed a sabre-blow at him to cut him down; but, as the murderous arm was poised above, Mr. Robertson stooped, and, raising his arm at the time, warded it off; the miscreant then rode off, being satisfied at this cut at the detested Nazarene.

Another ruffian seized one of his little girls, a pretty child of nine years old, and scratched her arm several times with his dagger, calling out *flous* (money) at each stroke. At the water-port, Mr. Robertson joined his fainting wife, and the British Consul and his wife, with Mr. Lucas and Mr. Allnut. An old Moor never deserted the Consul's family, "faithful among the faithless;" and a Jewess, much attached to the family, abandoned them only to return to those allied to her by the ties of blood.

Their situation was now still perilous, for, should they be discovered by the wild Berbers, they all might be murdered. This night, the 15th, was a most anxious one, and their apprehensions were dreadful. Dawn of day was fast approaching, and every hour's delay rendered their condition more precarious. In this emergency, Mr. Lucas, who never once failed or lost his accustomed suavity and presence of mind amidst these imminent dangers, resolved upon communicating with the fleet by a most hazardous experiment. On his way from the town-gate to the water-port, he noticed some deal planks near the beach. The idea struck him of turning these into a raft, which, supporting him, could enable their party to communicate with the squadron. Mr. Lucas fetched the planks, and resolutely set to work. Taking three of them, and luckily finding a quantity of strong grass cordage, he arranged them in the water, and with some cross-pieces, bound the whole together; and, besides, having found two small pieces of board to serve him as paddles, he gallantly launched forth alone, and, in about an hour, effected his object, for he excited the attention of the French brig, 'Canard,' from which a boat came and took him on board.

The officers, being assured there were no Moors on guard at the batteries, and that the Berbers were wholly occupied in plundering the city, promptly and generously sent off a boat with Mr. Lucas to the rescue of the alarmed and trembling fugitives. The Prince de Joinville afterwards ordered them to be conveyed on board the 'Warspite.' The self-devotedness, sagacity, and indefatigable exertions of the excellent young man, Mr. Lucas, were above all encomiums, and, at the hands of the British Government, he deserved some especial mark of favour.

Poor Mrs. Levy (an English Jewess, married to a Maroquine Jew), and her family were left behind, and accompanied the rest of the miserable Jews and natives, to be maltreated, stripped naked, and, perhaps, murdered, like many poor Jews. Mr. Amrem Elmelek, the greatest native merchant and a Jew, died from fright. Carlos Bolelli, a Roman, perished during the sack of the city.

Mogador was left a heap of ruins, scarcely one house standing entire, and all tenantless. In the fine elegiac bulletin of the bombarding Prince, "Alas! for thee, Mogador! thy walls are riddled with bullets, and thy mosques of prayer blackened with fire!" (or something like these words.)

## COMMERCE WITH MOROCCO.

### TANGIER.

Tangier trades almost exclusively with Gibraltar, between which place and this, an active intercourse is constantly kept up.

The principal articles of importation into Tangier are, cotton goods of all kinds, cloth, silk-stuffs, velvets, copper, iron, steel, and hardware of every description; cochineal, indigo, and other dyes; tea, coffee, sulphur, paper, planks, looking-glasses, tin, thread, glass-beads, alum, playing-cards, incense, sarsaparilla, and rum.

The exports consist in hides, wax, wool,

leeches, dates, almonds, oranges, and other fruit, bark, flax, durra, chick-peas, bird-seed, oxen and sheep, henna, and other dyes, woollen sashes, haicks, Moorish slippers, poultry, eggs, flour, &c.

The value of British and foreign goods imported into Tangier in 1856 was: British goods, £101,773 6s., foreign goods, £33,793.

The goods exported from Tangier during the same year was: For British ports, £63,580 10s., for foreign ports, £13,683.

The following is a statement of the number of British and foreign ships that entered and cleared from this port during the same year. Entered: British ships 203, the united tonnage of which was 10,883; foreign ships 110, the total tonnage of which was 4,780.

Cleared: British ships 207, the united tonnage of which was 10,934; foreign ships 110, the total tonnage of which was 4,780.

Three thousand head of cattle are annually

exported, at a fixed duty of five dollars per head, to Gibraltar, for the use of that garrison, in conformity with the terms of special grants that have, from time to time, been made by the present Sultan and some of his predecessors. In addition to the above, about 2,000 head are, likewise, exported annually, for the same destination, at a higher rate of duty, varying from eight dollars to ten dollars per head. Gibraltar, also, draws from this place large supplies of poultry, eggs, flour, and other kinds of provisions.

## MOGADOR.

From the port of Mogador are exported the richest articles the country produces, viz., almonds, sweet and bitter gums, wool, olive-oil, seeds of various kinds, as cummin, gingelen, aniseed; sheep-skins, calf, and goat-skins, ostrich-feathers, and occasionally maize.

The amount of exports in 1855 was: For British ports, £228,112 3s. 2d., for foreign ports, £55,965 13s. 1d.

The imports are Manchester cotton goods, which have entirely superseded the East India long cloths, formerly in universal use, blue salampores, prints, sugar, tea, coffee, Buenos Ayres slides, iron, steel, spices, drugs, nails, beads and deals, woollen cloth, cotton wool, and mirrors of small value, partly for consumption in the town, but chiefly for that of the interior, from Morocco and its environs, as far as Timbuctoo.

The amount of imports in 1855 was: British goods, £136,496 7s. 6d., foreign goods £31,222 11s. 5d.

The trade last year was greatly increased by the unusually large demand for olive-oil from all parts, and there is no doubt that, under a more liberal Government, the commerce might be developed to a vast extent.

## RABAT.

The principal goods imported at Rabat are, alum, calico of different qualities, cinnamon, fine cloth, army cloth, cloves, copperas, cotton prints, raw cotton, sewing cotton, cutlery, dimity, domestics, earthenware, ginger, glass, handkerchiefs (silk and cotton), hardware, indigo, iron, linen, madder root, muslin, sugar (refined and raw), tea, and tin plate.

The before-mentioned articles are imported partly for consumption in Rabat and Sallee, and partly for transmission into the interior.

The value of different articles of produce exported at Rabat during the last five years amounts to £34,860 1s.

There can be no doubt that the imports and exports at Rabat would greatly increase, if the present high duties were reduced, and Government monopolies abolished. Large quantities of hides were exported before they were a Government monopoly: now the quantity exported is very inconsiderable.

## MAZAGAN.

*Goods Imported.*—Brown Domestics, called American White, muslins, raw cotton, cotton-bales, silk and cotton pocket-handkerchiefs; tea, coffee, sugars, iron, copperas, alum; many other articles imported, but in very small quantities.

A small portion of the importations is consumed at Mazagan and Azimore, but the major portions in the interior.

The amonut of the leading goods exported in 1855 was:—Bales of wool, 6,410; almonds, 200 serons; grain, 642,930 fanegas.

No doubt the commerce of this port would be increased under better fiscal laws than those now established.

But the primary and immediate thing to be looked after is the wilful casting into the anchorage-ground of stone-ballast by foreigners. British masters are under control, but foreigners will persist, chiefly Sardinian masters.

THE END

LONDON:
Printed by A. Schulze, 13, Poland Street.

# MR. SKEET'S ANNOUNCEMENTS
## FOR THE FORTHCOMING SEASON.

### I.
### LITERARY REMINISCENCES AND MEMOIRS OF
## THOMAS CAMPBELL,
Author of "The Pleasures of Hope."
By his Friend and Coadjutor, CYRUS REDDING,
Author of "Fifty Years' Recollections, Literary and Personal."
2 Vols. with Portrait, 21s.

### II.
Posthumous Work by the celebrated African Traveller James Richardson.
## TRAVELS IN MOROCCO.
By the late JAMES RICHARDSON,
Author of "A Mission to Central Africa," "Travels in the Desert of Sahara."
EDITED BY HIS WIDOW.
2 Vols. profusely Illustrated, 21s.

### III.
## MY STUDY CHAIR;
### OR, MEMOIRS OF MEN AND BOOKS.
By the late D. O. MADDYN, ESQ.,
Author of "The Age of Pitt and Fox," "Chiefs of Parties," &c.
In 2 Vols. post 8vo., 21s.

### IV.
## FOUR YEARS IN BURMAH.
By W. H. MARSHALL, ESQ., late Editor of the "Rangoon Chronicle."
2 Vols. with Illustrations, 21s.

### V.
NEW NOVEL by the Author of "The Moors and the Fens."
## TOO MUCH ALONE.
By F. G. TRAFFORD,
Author of "The Moors and the Fens."
3 Vols. post 8vo.

### VI.
NEW NOVEL BY CYRUS REDDING.
## STOCKWELL HOUSE,
### OR KEEPING UP APPEARANCES.
By CYRUS REDDING,
Author of "Fifty Years' Recollections, Literary and Personal," &c.
3 Vols. post 8vo.

### VII.
NEW WORK ON ITALY.
## BEFORE THE DAWN,
### A TALE OF ITALY. A NOVEL.
By KATE CRICHTON.
2 Vols. post 8vo.

### VIII.
## LIBERTY HALL, OXON.
### A STORY OF COLLEGES.
By W. WINWOOD READE, ESQ.
3 vols. post 8vo.

# NEW EDITIONS.

## Second Edition of
## CHIEFS OF PARTIES,
### PAST AND PRESENT.
By D. O. MADDYN, ESQ., Author of "The Age of Pitt and Fox."
2 Vols. post 8vo., 21s.

"In all the book there is refreshment and agreeable illustration."—*Athenæum.*

"We predict for this work a permanent success. We admire the author much. His book is a capital repertoire of political information, and we can cordially recommend it."—*Literary Gazette.*

"May be conscientiously recommended as the very work for book clubs and readers anxious for a pleasant and trustworthy insight into the circle where the great and most active-minded men of our country 'live, move, and have their being.'"—*Manchester Advertiser.*

## Second Edition.
## FIFTY YEARS' RECOLLECTIONS,
### LITERARY AND PERSONAL,
WITH SKETCHES AND ANECDOTES OF ALMOST EVERY CELEBRATED CHARACTER OF THE PRESENT CENTURY.
By CYRUS REDDING. Second and Revised Edition, 3 vols.

Among many other individuals alluded to, are: Pitt—Sheridan—Porteous—Paull—Lord H. Petty—Herbert Compton—Spencer Smith—Sir Sidney Smith—Dr. Maclean—Davies Gilbert—Mrs. Wells—Col. Hanger—Major Topham—Mrs. Siddons—Dr. Wolcot—Lucien Bonaparte—General Tench—Sir A. Wellesley—Belzoni—Sir R. Calder—Lord Holland—Sir M. M. Lopez—General McCarthy—Lord Boringdon—Canning—Archdeacon Nares—Monk Lewis—Spencer Perceval—Angelica Catalani—J. Jekyl—Sir V. Gibbs—Thomas Hardy—Hewson Clarke—Lewis Goldsmith—Madame de Stael—Caleb Colton—Jew Hart—B. West—Col. Thornton—John Hunt—J. Demaria—Chevalier Canea—De Fredrique—David Wilkie—Talleyrand—Thistlewood—Louis XVIII.—Duchenois—Col. Hilpert—Potier—Du Roure—Meetelli—Lacepède—R. Heathcote—De Sodre—Bate Dudley—A. W. Schlegel—Dr. Parr—Major du Fay—Marshal Suchet—Van Prate—Count Porro—Sièyes—Santorre di Santa Rosa—Barry St. Leger—W. Roscoe—Sir C. Greville—H. Matthews—General Arabin—Madame du Four—Bishop of Toronto—J. Banim—A. Montemont—S. Rogers—Prior of La Trappe—L. Shiel—T. Barnes—J. Montgomery—W. Hazlitt—D. O'Connell—W. Irving—Earl Grey—Dunn Hunter—Judge Best—W. Graham—D. Cochrane—J. Galt—T. de Trueba—F. Hemans—Professor Wilson—T. Hood—Mrs. Shelley—General Torrijos—Sir W. Ouseley—Countess Guiccioli—J. G. Lockhart—Sen. Gorsatiza—J. Hogg—Sir J. Mackintosh—Sismondi—T. Campbell—Ugo Foscolo—T. N. Talfourd—Prince Czartorisky—Sir R. Peel—J. Niemcevitz—Scott—Lord Dillon—Marquis of Anglesey—Col. Pisa—Godfrey Higgins—J. Martin—B. Haydon—J. Clare—Sir C. Elkins—T. Pringle—General Miller—Sir C. Wolseley—Sen. La Gasca—Horace Smith—W. Beckford—Lord Western—Miss Mitford—Dr. Gall—Sir C. Morgan—General Pépe—Lord Torrington—Chevalier Pecchio—Blanco White—F. Marryat—B. D'Israeli—Countess of Blessington—Count D'Orsay, &c., &c.

## Second Edition.
## Memoirs of WILLIAM BECKFORD, of Fonthill,
Author of "VATHEK." In 2 vols. with fine portrait, 21s.

"The life of Beckford was worth writing, and the writer has unveiled the treasures of the pre-Adamite Sultans and their singular master to the gaze of a generation which had begun to forget all about him."—*Press.*

"Again, the lover of books, of paintings, of old china gems, and of all that is costly and rare, is referred to the book itself."—*Leader.*

"Contains matter of much interest, and is replete with anecdotes of that singular man himself, and of the illustrious circle of which he was a member."—*Observer.*

# NEW WORKS.

## PERSONAL MEMOIRS OF CHARLES THE SECOND,
With Sketches of his Court and Times.

By CAPT. CLAYTON, Author of "Letters from the Nile," "Ubique."
2 Vols. with Portrait, 21s.

"Well written, and the language plain and nervous, it pleasingly mingles light and interesting incidents with the dry pages of historical biography—as a readable book—as a work calculated to illustrate the man as well as the monarch, we recommend the perusal of these volumes."—*Morning Chronicle.*

## THE FRENCH IN AFRICA.
By CAPTAIN CAVE. One vol. 8vo. with Maps, 10s. 6d.

"We welcome this volume as a solid and valuable addition to modern history; and future historians will be grateful to Captain Cave for having brought within their reach, and dressed up in such attractive guise, the facts concerning the French campaigns in Africa."—*Critic.*

NEW WORK by the Author of "History and Political Philosophy of the Productive Classes," &c.

## WOMEN, Past and Present:
Their Social Vicissitudes, Single and Matrimonial Relations, Rights, Privileges, and Wrongs.

By JOHN WADE, Author of "The Cabinet Lawyer," &c.
1 Vol, price 10s, 6d,

Females of the Primitive Ages.
Greek and Roman Ladies.
Women of the Mediæval Period.
Females under the Tudors and Stuarts.
Modern Ladies, French and English.
Frenchwomen before the Revolution.
Englishwomen of the Eighteenth Century.

Oriental Civilization and the Degradation of Eastern Women.
Equality of the Sexes,
The Amative Passion.
Matrimony and Celibacy.
Divorce and Separations.
Rights, Privileges and Wrongs of Women. &c. &c.

Mr. S. W. FULLOM'S NEW WORK. In 2 Vols.

## THE HUMAN MIND:
### ITS ACQUIREMENTS AND HISTORY.
By the Author of "The Marvels of Science."

"A book more brilliant or more complete has not been often given to the public. 'The Human Mind' is one of those Works that will hold a perennial place in human memory."—*Observer.*

"A vast subject, popularly treated."—*Spectator.*

## OUR VETERANS OF 1854,
IN CAMP AND BEFORE THE ENEMY.
BY A REGIMENTAL OFFICER. 1 Vol. cloth bound, 10s 6d.

"A genuine Soldier's book, full of frankness and fire, and will prove a welcome guest in every regimental library."—*Daily News.*

"Possesses sterling merit; and it is this that has secured such a favourable reception to 'Our Veterans of 1854.'"—*United Service Magazine.*

1 Vol. Price 8s. 6d. bound.

## FRANK BERESFORD;
OR, LIFE IN THE ARMY.
BY CAPTAIN CURLING.

Contents:—The First Start to Join—First Day at Mess—Shakspeare in Scotland—The Barrack Room—The Commanding Officer's Breakfast—A Quarrel at Mess—The Duel—The Orders Read upon Parade—Mistress Macfarlane's Party—Lieutenant Damain—The Culprit—A Romance in Real Life—Captain Fidgettie—Storm and Wreck—The Oddest of all Oddities—The Practical Jokers—The Adjutant and the Awkward Squad—More Jokes—The Amateur Play—Mutiny and Murder—Adela Vere—A Troop Ship getting out to Sea, &c. &c. &c.

# NEW WORKS—Continued.

1 Vol., small 8vo.

## THE MISER LORD;

A Sequel to "Frank Beresford, or Life in the Army."

BY CAPT. CURLING, Author of "The Soldier of Fortune."

Contents: Old Stories over the Bottle—A Lesson to a Subaltern—The Kentish Boatmen—The Soldiers and the Lawyer—Auld Reekie—A Duel in the West Indies—The Miser Lord—Adela Vere—The Marquis and the Bumpkin—Love at first Sight—The Miser Lord again—The Miser grows worse and worse—The Lawyer's Clerk and the Peeress—An Engagement—The Outcast—The Housebreakers—The Strolling Players—The Miser's Daughter—The Hussars and the Actors—Strange Visitors—The Two Attorneys—Cheltenham—The Berkeley Hunt—Amateur Theatricals—A Ball at Cheltenham—The Wanderer—The Rival Beauties—A Visit to Ireland—The Defence of Ballyrackett—The 151st to the Rescue, &c. &c.

## REDMARSH RECTORY,

A NOVEL. By NONA BELLAIRS, Author of "Going Abroad," &c. 3 vols.

"Gracefully written, and shows a pure and devoted mind."—*Globe.*

## THE WORLD AND HIS WIFE;

OR, A PERSON OF CONSEQUENCE.

A Novel in 3 vols.

BY LADY BULWER LYTTON.

"A most clever production."—*Messenger.*

"Has evidences of an intense purpose, and will create a sensation, perhaps become the marked book of the season."—*Dispatch.*

"Often, in its not very common talent of expression, reminds one strangely of Thomas Carlyle."—*Leader.*

## THE RICH HUSBAND,

A NOVEL OF REAL LIFE.

In 3 Vols. By the Author of "The Ruling Passion."

"A vivacious and amusing story, sprinkled with happy hits against the flying follies of our generation."—*Leader.*

"A dashing novel, hit off with much fire and vehemence, dealing faithfully with the follies of mankind, and the eccentricities of society."—*Messenger.*

### Second Edition.

## THE RIVAL SUITORS.

In 3 Vols.

By Mrs. HUBBACK, Authoress of "The Wife's Sister," &c.

"A very good novel, the best with which Mrs. Hubback has favoured us; it is well written, carefully worked out, and very interesting."—*Athenæum.*

"The present season is begun well by the novelists. Mrs. Hubback has done perfect justice to herself in the story of the 'Rival Suitors.'"—*Examiner.*

"An interesting Circulating Library work."—*Spectator.*

"A good story, well told, and we can recommend it to novel readers as worth perusal."—*Globe.*

"The 'Wife's Sister' was a popular Novel. It was called for at the libraries, it was extensively read; it was a story of strong family interest. In the 'Rival Suitors' the interest is of a similar quality."—*Leader.*

"'The Rival Suitors' is a very stirring story, improving as it goes on. The latter portion of it is romantically dramatic, and proves that Mrs. Hubback can conceive and execute with graphic hardihood. She has chosen, as we said at the outset, a particular route in the world of fiction, and she passes throughout, without dallying by the way, rendering every step she takes attractive to the spectator."—*Observer.*

---

## WRITERS

*Of Voyages, Travels, Memoirs, Fiction, &c., are respectfully invited to favour the Publisher with an inspection of their Manuscripts intended for publication.*

CHARLES J. SKEET, PUBLISHER,

10, KING WILLIAM STREET, CHARING CROSS.

www.ingramcontent.com/pod-product-compliance
Lightning Source LLC
Chambersburg PA
CBHW060657170426
43199CB00012B/1832